KUNG FU

CINEMA OF VENGEANCE

To: Richard Seyza

Remember no matter how
much you love the
Martial Arts. Family
come first.

Your friend

Sensei

Emilio Parriga

July 3, 1980

Bruce Lee

KUNG FU
CINEMA OF VENGEANCE

Verina Glaessner

Bounty Books

Designed by Peter Warne Associates

Copyright © 1974 by Lorrimer Publishing, Limited
Library of Congress Catalog Card Number: 74-81686
All rights reserved.
This Edition is published by Bounty Books
a division of Crown Publishers Inc.
by arrangement with Lorrimer Publishing Limited

ISBN 0-517-518317

Made and printed in Great Britain by
Lowe & Brydone (Printers) Ltd., Thetford, Norfolk

CONTENTS

ACKNOWLEDGEMENTS

The author wishes to thank all those who gave of their time to throw light on the darker corners of the subject of this book. Especial thanks are due to Run Run Shaw and Raymond Chow, who allowed themselves to be interviewed; David Chiang, Angela Mao, Huang Feng, Chu Yuan, who all took time off from hectic schedules to enlighten me about the production side of the kung fu industry; King Hu for his hospitality; and innumerable other people both in Hong Kong and London whose patience was regularly taxed with seemingly insoluble problems; the following companies for making films available for viewing and for allowing us to reproduce stills from the films they produced or distribute: Anglo-EMI, Cathay Films, Columbia-Warner, Eagle Films, Ember, Excelsior, Golden Era, Golden Harvest, Miracle, Shaw Brothers, and Twentieth Century Fox.

Where alternative or American titles of films exist, these are indicated in parentheses after the more usual title.

1. Ornate Choreographies of Violence

'What future is there in being born a Chinaman? You are born, eat your way through a handful of rice and you die!'
Shanghai Express

The wave of Chinese action films that quickly became known as 'kung fu' movies, or in the trade 'chop sockies', and the onslaught they made on the box-office charts of the world, was both unforeseen and unexpected. Led by *King Boxer*, (*Five Fingers of Death*, 1971) and hotly followed by the films of Bruce Lee that were to give the wave its sole superstar and cult martyr, these films set the scene for a mass invasion of western cinemas by Chinese action films.

The films all hinged on extremely skilfully shot, elongated fight sequences that opened up a whole new perspective on the term 'balletic violence'. Although the protagonists might use knives or swords, chains or even occasionally guns, such technology came a long way behind the visually-involving way they used their bodies in a series of nicely judged blocks, kicks, and jabs punctuated by massive leaps and backed by a soundtrack of shrieks and groans. The screen was alive with an ornate choreography of violence that exploited the dance-like postures of traditional Chinese martial arts – a mixture of boxing, wrestling and kick fighting. It was exotic.

King Boxer (1971).

The Killer (1971).

The Pirate (1972).

Gone was the rigid monolithic close-up of the television-influenced thriller. Gone, too, the all-pervasive, tortuous self-hatred, middle-aged disillusionment and sheer moral blackness that marked much of Hollywood's staple action output in the early seventies. The Chinese cinema was young, and it offered a world of diagrammatic moral clarity.

In this context the hero or heroine might well lose the battle but never the war. The characters that the stars create do not come by their last-reel triumph easily . . . the fights are always deadly and always, in the last analysis, with an opponent of worthy skills. Or at least of sufficient skills for him to put up a fight.

The rights for Chinese martial arts films that could a year earlier have been picked up for a song were going for handsomely rounded figures in 1973. They broke records wherever they showed. And it was not only the United States and Europe that was affected: *The New One-armed Swordsman* broke records in

Ten Fingers of Steel (1973): Wang Yu.

South America and *The Big Boss* packed them in in Beirut. European film studios emptied. The Italian film industry was seriously affected. Carlo Ponti was driven to resuscitate his popular superhero from costume epic days, Hercules, and launch him in a series of imitation kung fu films, starting with *Mr Hercules Against Karate*. Others followed suit.

Hollywood sat up and took notice. Warner Brothers launched into a co-production, the first equal co-production deal between a Chinese company and a Hollywood major. Hammer, Britain's highly successful home-grown horror unit, quit the parlous production situation in Britain to draw up a programme of two films to be made as co-productions with the Asian film industry's moguls – the Shaw brothers.

What increasingly astounded observers from the trade was the tiny outlay the films required and the giant profits they returned with the kind of inevitability the studios of the West had forgotten about since the coming of television. *The Big Boss* (*Fists of Fury*, 1971) cost a mere $100,000, yet took half a million in its home market before even beginning to count the profits raked in from abroad. *Fist of Fury* (*The Iron Hand*, 1972) cost $200,000 and grossed a million. *The New One-armed Swordsman* walked off with $250,000 – only $50,000 short of its total cost – after only two weeks in Hong Kong: it then went on to out-take *The Godfather* in some countries. It was all very different from the situation in the West, where the major companies were increasingly gearing themselves to banking on super-productions that would then take a year before even beginning to go into profit, where the total amount invested in films was in any case shrinking, and where the profits were increasingly re-invested thankfully in financially sounder areas than the hazardous area of film production.

What seemed to be happening was that the West was picking up on what may turn out to be the tailpiece of a South-east Asian movie boom of unparalleled proportions. The key to the success of an empire like that of the Shaw Brothers and of a plethora of mini-companies changing names and personnel on an almost film-to-film basis depended on a single factor . . . attendance figures. Hong Kong-made films had a vast audience stretching in a belt from Hong Kong down to the Philippines, Malaya and Indonesia. In Hong Kong itself, attendance reached an all-time high of 98,538,037 in 1966, and even if the figure had declined to some 71 million by 1973 this still looks supremely healthy.

The films also had low production costs. Hong Kong has no union problems for the simple reason that it doesn't have any unions. (There is, in fact, a film editors union, but that is persuasively shrugged aside.) Films could, and still can, be made in Hong Kong, Taiwan, Korea, Thailand for budgets that, including building and striking the set and advertising, still do not come even knee-high to those in Europe and America.

It didn't matter at first that the films arrived on the world market carelessly dubbed, hampered by an almost wilfully eclectic selection of library sound tracks (*Shaft* was one favourite, *Once Upon a Time in the West* another), stylistically hampered further by repeated use of back projections and studio lots which the set-dresser barely had time to alter from film to film; or that the characterizations were minimal, relationships one-dimensional and the plots, as one critic put it, 'dozed in their traces'.

The human weapon had arrived (and it arrived most flamboyantly in the person of Bruce Lee) – the country boy or girl who waived the unspoken rules, unmasked the head of the heroin gang, and smashed it in a way no one had hoped to see. Performers like Bruce Lee and Angela Mao altered the image of the Chinese for Western audiences.

Fist of Fury (1972).

Enter the Dragon (1973): Bruce Lee.

Hap Ki Do (1971).

The Mysterious Dr Fu Manchu (1929).

Redefining the West's traditional bogey man as hero was a notable coup. The cliché of the 'yellow menace' had prowled through Western cinema from silent days – the films made in Germany, for instance, suggestively close to the time when that country lost its Chinese concessions: *Der Fremde*, or Robert Reinert's *Opium*, or Fritz Lang's *Der Spinnen*, or the eight full-length episodes of *Die Herrin Der Welt*. Or the chorus that was taken up at the end of the First World War in Hollywood when the Chinese immigration raised the spectre of a very basic chauvinistic fear. A flood of films appeared in which the ultimate horror was revealed as being mixed marriage – something that had to be sidestepped even if the only alternative was death. There were serials like *The Yellow Menace*, films like *The Red Lantern* in which no less a star than Nazimova (playing a part-Chinese) found herself unable to marry her true love – race stood in her way. Titles like *Mandarin's Gold* and *The Yellow Arm*

streamed out of the studios. Lon Chaney appeared as Yen Sin in *Shadows* and Constance Talmadge was granted a last minute reprieve in *East is West* – she is revealed to be white after all in the last reel. And of course there is the film that provoked a riot when it was shown in Shanghai shortly after its completion – *Shanghai Express*, in which the Chinese form an undifferentiated backdrop for von Sternberg's 'real' European characters and 'real' Eurasian villain. The image reaches forward in fact through Warner Oland's 1929 Fu Manchu in *The Mysterious Dr Fu Manchu* (directed by Rowland V. Lee) to Christopher Lee's sanguine interpretation of this shady manipulator of men in the later series, including the 1966 film *Brides of Fu Manchu*, to Bond's *Dr No*. The shift is probably most succinctly illustrated by the co-opting of a literal 'son of Fu Manchu' – a Chinese American – into the retinue of comic book 'Avenger' heroes.

The Mysterious Dr Fu Manchu.

It seems entirely appropriate that the wave of Chinese films that found a responsive audience in the West took for their centrepiece fight techniques that had unofficially been designated as 'acceptable for bad guys only' by Hollywood, and enacted them with such dynamism that it seemed as if the average western brawl would never be able to hold attention again. The basis for the success of the kung fu films in the States was the same ghetto audience that carried the wave of 'black' Hollywood action films a year or so previously – something confirmed by Hollywood's instant businesslike synthesizing of the two genres in a series of black karate thrillers. Fred Weintraub and Paul Heller followed up their co-production with Bruce Lee's company Concord, with *Black Belt Jones*, for instance, a film whose plot hinged on the attack by Mafia gangmen on a black 'youth work' orientated karate school. Elsewhere, the films showed to receptive audiences on a similar beat to that awarded to Italian westerns in the mid 'sixties. In common with both the westerns and the 'black' films, Chinese kung fu films could be seen to have a social core to them, even if it was a social core transmuted – and sometimes with amazing boldness – into simplified fist-waving or swordtoting melodrama.

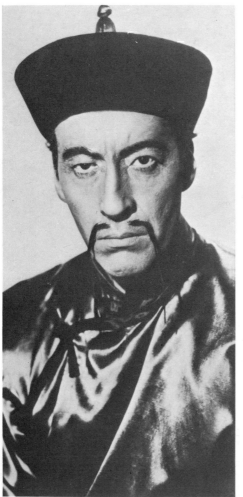

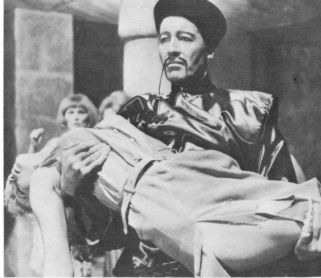

Brides of Fu Manchu (1966).

2. The Arena

'We were told this was a worthwhile town but it doesn't seem that way', kung fu performer and acrobat with a travelling medicine show. Man steps forward: 'Don't you know the rules? Mr Chow owns this town.' Mr Chow steps forward – he is wearing silk and toying with an ivory cigarette holder.
He Walks Like a Tiger (King of Kung Fu)

Kung fu films are poverty row cinema, generally critically despised and berated for what is seen as their sensationalistic concentration on violent action at the expense of such comfortable attributes as character development, nuance and even narrative tension.

'How would you define your audience?', I asked a Shaw Brothers employee. 'There are a lot of poor people, a lot of illiterate people in Hong Kong . . . they go to the films,' came the reply. These are the films that are made and shown in the ninety-seven cinemas of a Hong Kong still embarrassed by the cold-blooded contrast between its central skyscrapers and the 300,000 people who live in squatter huts, temporary housing or on the old resettlement estates that have degenerated into hideous slum blocks terrorised by criminal gangs. Ninety-nine per cent of the population of this British administered colony are Cantonese speaking Chinese and some four million of them are crammed into an area of less than 400 square miles. Fifty-five per cent of the population is under 25. A permanent land boom escalates rents. There is a serious drug addiction problem. Welfare provisions are inadequate. There is a high illiteracy rate and it is still permissible for parents to keep a child away from school if real financial need can be shown. A ten-hour day and a six-day week are usual. A reputable magazine estimated some ten per cent of Hong Kong's gross national product to come from corrupt practices, mainly from the big three – gambling, prostitution and drugs. Not surprisingly, violent crime increased some 218 per cent between 1968 and 1972.

The territories that make up the Mandarin circuit hardly come off any better; through Taiwan, Thailand, Korea, Singapore the picture is depressingly similar, a tale of prevalent illiteracy, outlawed strikes, a poverty stricken peasantry still locked in a feudal agricultural system, and a continued drift by the young and uneducated but hopeful to cities that seem paved with gold, but that are ill equipped to take them.

The key factor is an acknowledged growing gap between rich and poor. In Singapore the price of rice has doubled, and in Hong Kong the Chinese population is decidely cynical about the British Government's willingness to stem spiralling living costs.

In a situation where a real-life Mr Big, the Golden Triangle opium king, was recently caught despite the efforts of his private army, and a revolt in Thailand exposed corruption in high places that encompassed gross extortion and opium dealing, worry about the violence in the films becomes academic.

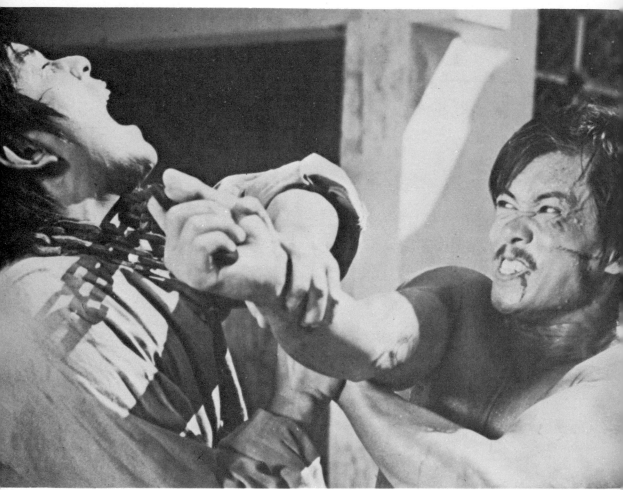

Kung Fu the Headcrusher (1973).

From the Highway (1970).

Bus Stop (1970).

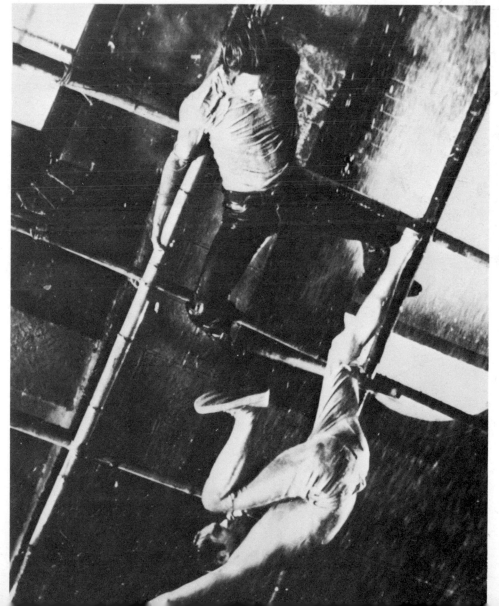

3. A Thousand Ways to Die

'In this world of guns and knives wherever Tang Lung goes he will walk alone.'
Bruce Lee's epitaph for Tang Lung, the character he plays in *Way of the Dragon*

The kind of action that became known in the West as 'kung fu' added a new dimension to the iconography of violence. It provided a more or less lethal-cum-balletic dance of resistance and conquest that threw away the rule book and had absolutely no truck with avoiding taboo regions of the opponent's body; groin kicks and eye gouges were simply part of the repertoire. Perhaps paradoxically, it could, when displayed at its most competent, express every shade of resentment, wiliness and sheer ingenuity. The resistance, which was always against enormous odds as a matter of course, carried all the implications of the unleashing of a natural force. In the context of a Hollywood movie world in which the protagonists seemed to be becoming noticeably more compromised, older and increasingly disillusioned, the dance of revenge fascinated. The fascination continued, as the West discovered the rationale behind a scheme of things that so blatantly brought the body back to the centre of things in a mode that time and again had the one winning against the many in the environment of gun and dagger-drawn back-alley ambushes as often as amid the studio exotica of China's remote past.

The words 'kung fu' in fact have no meaning beyond 'technique' or 'skill'. It is a phrase that can be applied to anyone's skill in any field, although it has become applied specifically to the field of Chinese martial arts, fighting skills which derived from various sources during China's Middle Ages.

One legend has the monks teaching the once-warring villages whom they had disarmed the techniques as a means of self-defence. The arts were granted their own deity during the Ming dynasty, when the legendary Chinese folk hero Kuan Ti was deified as the god of war, albeit a war god with a difference – symbolising, justice, loyalty and the traditions of the honourable warrior, he had the ability to avert war and protect people from its horrors. His statue, incidentally, presides over the 'black' martial arts museum in which Lee confronts Han in *Enter the Dragon*. There is usually a shrine to him in most martial arts schools.

Kung Fu the Headcrusher.

Blood Brothers (1972).   *Enter the Dragon.*

Paradoxically, to Western eyes, the core of the classic martial arts credo is a philosophy of patience: 'Avoid rather than check, check rather than force, force rather than injure, injure rather than maim, maim rather than kill.' And a key moment in any number of martial arts films is the particular point at which the protagonist, having deliberately restrained him or herself in an attempt to avoid confrontation with the enemy, still finds him spoiling for a fight . . . a point at which the most arcane and deadly skills are dusted off in preparation for a fight to the death. It is a moment that has been expected – and there is yet to be the film in which the sword is unequivocally replaced in the scabbard, or the hatchet buried.

Bruce Lee always made the claim that everything he did in his films was real: he made no use of trampolines or trick photography. Most other on-screen fights, however, are real only in the sense that most of the well-known performers have undergone training in one or other of the martial arts techniques. 'You have to know how to hold your hands, where to kick to, how to give out all your energy and yet avoid hurting your partner. If you do not know the martial arts you end up looking very ugly,' David Chiang 'The New One-armed Swordsman' explained.

Grace is a key word in relation to the martial arts on film and it seems entirely consonant with this that the basic moves are based on a study and interpretation of the fight techniques of animals, the praying mantis, the grasshopper, the white crane, the horse. . . . Hand forms are based on postures that imitate the tiger's claw, the crane's beak, and so on. And all this is allied to a detailed and accurate knowledge of human anatomy. Mastery of the martial arts is a long process involving meditation, breathing control and sustained discipline. It teaches increased

The New One-armed Swordsman (1970).

Enter the Dragon.

The Game of Death (1973).

perceptiveness, stoicism in the face of extremes and the ability to walk soundlessly; while the 'perfect master' has from early in Chinese history been credited with any number of almost supernatural powers: he is said to be able to walk through walls and to sense and counter a potential attack before the first move has been made. The art of 'kung fu' stretches in fact beyond the more visible fight techniques and into the fabric of Chinese culture. Born from the twin influences of Taoism and Buddhism, the martial arts stand as a practical application of these philosophies . . . with fighting forms becoming, ideally, simply vehicles towards a higher goal.

To Western eyes, the weaponry attached to the martial arts contest often looks either simple-minded or simply exotic. But such weapons as the two sectional staff, the *nanchaku*, used with skill, can attain a speed of 150 mph along its perimeter. The awkward-looking three sectional staff can function as a heavy club, twin sticks or a pole that, effectively, goes round corners. . . . As in the case of the twin butterfly swords, sticks and staves, daggers and the whole repertoire of more fanciful weaponry that is displayed in Shaw Brothers' costume films, the effectiveness comes from the skill of the wielder.

The martial arts are also an industry: the number of people taking some kind of martial arts course has swelled dramatically over the past few years: in America it has reached some ten million. Schools have opened on a more or less crash-course basis both there, in Britain and in Australia. Martial arts magazines have sprung up. There are postal order services dealing in kung fu clothes, shoes, practice protectors, and, less traditionally, Bruce Lee tee-shirts, buttons and jackets. Not to mention those expensive send-away weapon services and their fully illustrated catalogues listing such implements as bladed chains.

Looked at one way, this suggests a minor revolution in countries supposedly dedicated to the ideology behind team games and the value of sheer largeness (in kung fu movies the losers are normally bigger and distinctly tougher-looking than the winners). In their place is a ritual primarily involving a personal discipline tied to a generalized concept of justice and loyalty to the weak. This concept is so generalized in fact, that it can appear to tie in equally with the tenets of the ritualized forms of gangsterism, as much as with liberal concepts of social responsibility. The martial arts may be like an iceberg with nine-tenths stretching back into the roots of Chinese culture, but to the West there is another attraction. Martial arts magazines make a point of the fact that the arts may well make a good keep-fit routine, but they can also kill. The attraction there can be in this playing with fire element comes through loud and clear: how to have your meditational-spiritual cake and eat it too. It is suggestive that the rise of martial arts in America should coincide with the current gun craze. It is interesting also that it should arise in a country that has historically had long contact with Korea, China and South-east Asia, generally through a series of disastrous and traumatic conflicts.

Below is a run-down of some of the forms of martial arts most commonly featured on film with a brief description of each:

Hap ki do or *Aikido:* it makes use of the principle of deflecting the attacker's energy against him or her self. It turns up as the key motif in the film of the same name in which Angela Mao, a real life second degree black belt *hap ki do* expert defends the honour of her school.

Fist of Fury.

Enter the Dragon.

Jeet kune do: means 'fist-intercepting-way'; the method used in all Bruce Lee's films. He arrived at it from choice among a wide range of sources. Lee researched into biomechanics, examined muscle function in detail and taught concentration on the upsetting of the opponent's centre of gravity. He concentrated on developing rotary movements as an economical way of using energy to most effect – as in his famous series of three continuous roundhouse kicks. He developed a high velocity internal punch technique that left little external mark but that set up a series of vibrations in the body that could result in internal haemorrhaging. He was preoccupied with the idea of fighting taller and bigger people than himself (he was five-foot-four), and took this to greatest lengths in *The Game of Death* in which he confronts a seven-foot basket-ball hero. He had a vast book library on the martial arts, and an equally vast library of film of fight tournaments, including film of children's tournaments, as he found that children often attain a useful state of relaxation. Lee obsessively built everything he knew about the martial arts back into films in which he often staged fights with his own pupils (Bob Baker in *Fist of Fury*, for instance). Criticized by conventional schools for its eclecticism and lack of philosophical base *jeet kune do* nevertheless did provide the most visually expressive kung fu style of all.

Lee had found Chinese film 'unreal . . . all that jumping around all the time'. He convinced his director Lo Wei to do away with the weaponry and trick effects that Chinese films to that point had relied on and instead used his body alone to express all the force and control necessary.

Judo: derived from *jujitsu* (a back-up technique used by Japanese swordsmen). It was adapted in the late 19th century primarily as a means of overcoming tall oponents and evolved into a

Blood Brothers.

The Shadow Boxer (1973).

Kung Fu (1973).

system of sport and defence incorporating a code of humanitarian ethics. Again, simply occurring as a fight technique wielded by the skilled, usually Japanese, opponent in the bulk of Chinese action films.

Karate: means empty hand. Modern karate can be traced to Okinawa, although its roots go back to Chinese boxing. An attribute of villainy in the films, it provides a good fight before being effectively trounced.

Shaolin boxing: close to *tai chi* with training similarly focusing on the development of consciousness of the 'chi' or life-force, a central concept of taoism, but concentrating more on muscle power and force. It probably penetrated most people's consciousness with the coming of the television series *Kung Fu* in which David Carradine plays Kwai Chang Caine, an exile from a Shaolin Temple wandering through the American West. The film interlaces sequences of Caine's temple training with sequences illustrating his attempts to put his learning to use in his new environment and is more notable for its visually super, evocative temple scenes and its capturing of part of the essence of the philosophy behind the arts, than for its palpably faked action. It is notable also for its use of an eclectic array of aphorisms.

Taekwondo: an early form of the art developed in Korea at the end of the 6th century A.D., but it was only officially formalised in the mid-fifties by a retired major in the Korean army. Translated literally, the name means 'art of hand and foot fighting', and, as this suggests, it involves the application of punches, flying kicks, blocks, dodges and interceptions with the arms, hands and feet, to the rapid destruction of the enemy. Used extensively in Korea by the army, police and notorious Korean C.I.A., it is often taken up by American army units stationed there. It has also been recommended for use by women

When Taekwondo Strikes (1973).

Blood Brothers.

as it relies less on massive arm muscles and more on leg work.

Tai Chi Chuan: the Chinese say that whoever practises *tai chi* correctly will gain the pliability of a child, the health of a lumberjack and the peace of mind of a sage. Although other Asian methods stress the yielding principle, none achieve the same degree of relaxation and subtlety. The name is derived from the Chinese meaning 'supreme ultimate' and it is based on the *yin* and *yang* principles. Involving slow, harmonious, circular movements, it is the least aggressive of the arts. To quote from the *Tai Chi Chuan* classic manuscript: 'When your opponent brings pressure to your left side that side should be empty. The same holds for your right side. When he pushes upwards or downwards against you, he feels as if there is no end to the emptiness he encounters. When he advances against you, he feels the distance is incredibly long; when he retreats he feels it is exasperatingly short.' The passage expresses perfectly the sense of the unreal, the supernatural, that the best of the

Golden Swallow (1969).

kung fu films attempt to duplicate: the the fight against an enemy who refuses to be pinned down through the normal cut and thrust of conflict. A key exponent of the art is Run Run Shaw himself, who does an hour of practice every morning.

Wing Chun Kung Fu: 'lightning fast'. A non-traditional method supposed to have been founded by a Buddhist nun in the 17th century who dispensed with the elaborate poses and stances of traditional methods, substituting instead a close-range style whose main features are economy of movement, directness of action and a unique kind of straight punch that can severely injure from a distance as short as six inches. Practised mainly in Hong Kong, it has recently spread to the United States and Australia. Bruce Lee learnt this technique in Hong Kong and acknowledged his debt to it. The *wing chun* exponent is taught to move in constantly towards his opponent. He also specialises in a low kick in which the focus of the force becomes the heel, and the target the shin, the kneecap, groin or kidneys. It is nothing if not direct and aggressive.

Bandits from Shantung (1971).

4. The Producers

'We have a little sex, we have a little comedy, we have mysteries, dramas . . . and as long as people go to a certain kind of film we will keep making them. Moviemakers after all make movies to the wishes of the people.
Run Run Shaw

Between 1970 and 1973 roughly 200 films were produced annually in Hong Kong and Taiwan. At least, that is the number submitted for censorship. There are tales of warehouses full of un-released and unsold kung fu quickies permanently shelved. Of the films released, about thirty to forty a year came from Shaw Brothers and some dozen or so from Golden Harvest. If Shaw Brothers has the size, the output, the organization of a 'thirties Holly-wood studio, then Golden Harvest has perhaps the gimcrack entrepreneurial enterprise of its 'twenties predecessor. Golden Harvest present a one-man success story on a Hollywoodesque scale. Shaw Brothers boasts one of the largest privately-owned film studios in the world and has built up a pervasive, uncrackable mystique as well. In fact the aura of antique Hollywood revisited is compounded by such small details as the Shaw Brothers insignia – the initials SB against a shield – remarkably similar to the old Warner Brothers logo. The films that have received world-wide distribution have come from these two companies.

Shaws' Movietown, located on the Kowloon-New Territories enclave of the China mainland, boasts ten sound stages, sixteen exterior sets, a gallery of accurately reproduced costumes from every conceivable period of China's past. It has its own dormitory blocks for stars and studio staff, a workshop com-plex and a continuous shooting schedule that allows seven films to be completed simultaneously. They employ a staff of 1,500 and have a chain of cinemas that extends from Hong Kong through South-east Asia. In 1973 they released thirty films; four of them took over one million Hong Kong dollars at the box office. Run Run Shaw is chairman and one of the world's richest men. His personal wealth runs to four houses, a villa on the studio backlot, a slab of property interests, a clutch of Swiss bank accounts, and another handful of mansions in Singapore where the com-pany has another studio (there is a third in Kuala Lumpur). His brother Run Me controls distribution in Singapore and his son Vee King is an executive on the board of the company.

The Shaw family entered film-making in the 'twenties when Run Run's father foreclosed a mortgage on a theatre and brother Runji saw in the foreclosure a useful opportunity to stage a play he had written. The play did not exactly draw the crowds, but a film version which the brothers shot with a handcranked French camera had more success. It was Shanghai in the early 'twenties, a time when silent films – especially American ones – were making all the running. The Shaw brothers began to tout films around the villages of the Malay Peninsula. Cinema was going through the first of the Chinese industry's boom periods with some hundred studios already in action in Shanghai. In 1924 the brothers moved to Singapore and set up a com-pany to distribute the films of Fairbanks, Pickford and Chaplin. They also began to piece together a chain of some hundred cinemas and amusement parks. Their next coup was during the slump.

Run Run Shaw.

They began to buy up theatres and, in the face of general disbelief, to equip them for sound. Their expansive projects were halted when their theatre chain was confiscated by the Japanese during the war.

Hong Kong provided a refuge for Chinese film makers fleeing first the Japanese, then the Kuomintang and later, after the People's Liberation Army took Peking, the Communists. 'Underground' cinema of various shades flourished, all competing for the same local and overseas Chinese market. After the war it was the Hong Kong film industry that was the first to recover.

The Shaw brothers moved to Hong Kong. They acquired the rights to the films of a handful of the most important American majors. At this time, there were four main studios and a handful of tiny refugee companies that regularly worked a twenty-four-hour shift, turning out films that ran through their possible audience in a matter of weeks. It wasn't unheard of for studios to be financed from profits made from gambling and prostitution rackets. Film was booming despite an almost total lack of professional standards. Some three hundred films a year were being made. This was the environment within which Shaws began to pick up the traces of Shanghai film-making, turning out remakes of the historical spectacles that had rocketed that industry to unprecedented popularity. By the end of the 'fifties, Shaws had rebuilt their cinema chain and shortly afterwards established the Shaw Brothers spectacle formula. By the mid-sixties Shaws had reached a watershed of sorts with a chain of 127 cinemas, a handful of amusement parks, and three film studios – a verticle integration that sped their race to the top. They also began to cast their eye towards the world market.

Up to 1959 Run Run Shaw had been in Singapore looking after distribution, while his brother Rundi was in charge of production in Hong Kong.

'We started really,' Run Run Shaw explains, 'in 1959. Up to then we had only a very small studio as a branch unit. In 1959 I came from Singapore and began to build the studio up to what it is today. It was then that we began production on a proper scale. At first we made very low budget black and white films, then in 1962 we had our first colour musical success. In fact we had a series of hits that included *The Kingdom and the Beauty* (a romantic

The Kingdom and the Beauty (1960).

love story set in dynastic China about the thwarted love of an Emperor for a country girl), and *Eternal Love* (another period story which has the lovers re-united after death). This broke all records for Chinese films. When I took over in 1958, films were of very poor quality. I was looking after distribution, so I could see at first hand that they were not doing well. In my experience it was the good film that people went to, whether Chinese or not. So I thought that if we were to make better films with bigger budgets it must bring the crowds, then people would want to see Chinese films, for in those days people thought that Chinese films would never really pay. My theory was that only the quality needed improving. And it was with this idea in mind that I came to Hong Kong. And the results proved me right. Today I can say that the gross theatrical takings for Chinese films are higher than that for imported films.

'At first we shot the films on very long schedules – labour conditions were more in our favour then and we could afford longer schedules, and also we were less experienced than we are now. Now, although it is wrong to say that we make films quickly, we are trying to speed up the schedules so that we spend some forty-five to seventy shooting days on a film.'

Their policy is to make a variety of kinds of films (rarely spending more than $300,000 per film) and then when a certain kind reveals itself to be out-taking the others to make more of them to supply the demand. 'We started making swordfight films in 1964 and the action film became very popular, so we made more, until in the late 'sixties half our annual output was action films. The action film that you call the kung fu movie developed from the traditional swordfight film around 1964, and then later, in 1968, we made the first film that could be called a kung fu film – *The One-armed Swordsman*. But the trend

Eternal Love (1962).

The One-armed Swordsman (1968).

to action was not confined to Asia. Hollywood made Westerns for years, the Italian studios took them over, putting in more violence and more emotion as they did, so that the Hollywood films became less popular . . . and before that there were those Hercules films, and then the James Bond films, and modern-day war films. And now there is the Chinese martial arts action film. People go to the theatre for a little excitement and of course for something new, and for the Western audience the Chinese action film is new. For how long? That is a different question. But for as long as they go to a certain kind of film we will keep making them, movie-makers after all make movies to the wishes of the people. After all we do not make one kind of film . . . we have a little sex, we have a little comedy, we have mysteries, dramas, and now there are our co-productions with Carlo Ponti, with Frank Kramer on *This Time I'll Make You Rich*, and with Hammer . . . so we will see how these films go in their different parts of the world. I am sure people will go for anything new . . . and I believe I am right.'

Illicit Desire (1973).

Legends of Lust (1973).

In the late 'sixties/early 'seventies two of Shaws' chief executives left to go independent: Ricky Uy left to start Panasia films (which made *The Opium Trail* with Angela Mao), and Raymond Chow, Shaws' second-in-command, left to form what has become known as the kung fu company *par excellence* – Golden Harvest. Raymond Chow discovered a nineteen-year-old Chinese opera star named Angela Mao Ying and signed her up and then went on after a year of bargaining, along with nearly every other company in Hong Kong, to sign Bruce Lee . . . and thereby hangs a small fortune.

The 200,000 square feet of Golden Harvest's studio straggle up a near vertical hillside off Hammer Hill Road. The offices are plain, if not bleak. The contrast with Shaws is absolute. In a little over two years, Golden Harvest has made itself into the second largest production company in South-east Asia, starting out with modest hired studios in the New Territories and taking over their current spot in late 1971. Since then their films have been known to break box-office records previously held by *The Sound of Music*. In 1973 they had units making films in San Francisco, Korea and Taiwan as well as keeping their Kowloon studios busy. To date, their main interest has been in action films, laced perhaps, as their current assessment of the market would have it, with sex, comedy or a sprinkling of European faces. 'These guys,' commented a somewhat disenchanted European actor lending international appeal to a new action piece, 'just measure the fight sequences by the foot and then make the script with the longest fight sequences.' If rehearsal for dialogue is minimal or plain non-existent, the fight scenes are planned, rehearsed and shot exactingly, after much discussion between the fight instructor, the actors and the director.

Raymond Chow was born in Hong

Raymond Chow.

Kong and spent his childhood there. His father was a banker and in 1939, as he wanted his son to have a Chinese education, the family moved to Shanghai. The Japanese started the attack on Pearl Harbour a year later and they were more or less stranded there. He finished college in Shanghai just before the Communists took it over in 1949. 'I had studied journalism at the American Christian university in Shanghai and in my last semester I worked part time for United Press, in addition to running my own English and Chinese school papers. When I came to Hong Kong I joined the Hong Kong *Standard* and won a scholarship to study at the University of Missouri, but I had my family to support. My father had died and my two younger brothers hadn't finished school, so I gave that up. Newspaper work didn't pay too well so I had several part-time jobs. Then I joined the 'Voice of America' and stayed with them for about seven years

setting up their radio and motion-picture production section catering for Chinese communities overseas. In 1958 one of my professors had introduced me to Run Run Shaw, mentioning that Shaw was about to start his operation in Hong Kong and was looking for an advertising and publicity manager. I decided to take the job. It was a big challenge . . . Shaw was known to be a very tough boss. It was two months later that I saw the first film they produced. I was horrified and told him I wanted to quit. I felt so appalled I felt sure I couldn't sell the film. Shaw replied, "Well, that's exactly why I had to come and take over production . . . because they are so bad." So that's how I got into production. And I still had the advertising and publicity job.' Chow's name appears on at least one of the big budget extravaganzas of the period, the vastly successful *Magnificent Concubine*, otherwise known as *Yang Kwei Fei*, which starred Li Li-hua and

Yang Kwei Fei (The Magnificent Concubine) (1962).

won a prize at the Cannes Festival in 1962 for its production values. Interestingly, in common with the other Shaw mainstream Mandarin large budgeted efforts at this time, this film was essentially a remake of a traditional Chinese opera, and for the 1954 version no less a director than Mizoguchi had been brought over from Japan to direct. Shaws' version was directed by Li Han-hsiang – effectively, by all accounts. So Raymond Chow helped Shaw set up the Clearwater Bay studio: 'We started out with just two stages, then added two more, then four more to that . . . we bought a huge hangar and converted that to four sound stages . . . I worked with him for eleven and a half years and the films we made were very successful, making Shaws the largest entertainment empire . . . it is history. Then we

had some differences of opinion on the future of Chinese films. I felt that it was time the Hong Kong film industry stepped in and started supplying the world market, as other film centres around the world were suffering severe economic crises. I started Golden Harvest in May 1970 and so far we have produced forty films. . . . At the moment, we are producing a lot of *won ton* Westerns, as they are called, but I think that particular tide will pass very shortly. What will be left will be a market for the better of the Hong Kong films. Now the door is open, it is easier for distributors to be receptive to the idea of Chinese films. You have no idea of the trouble we ran into when we first started to push our films overseas. The reaction was: "What! A Chinese film!" Then Bruce Lee changed all that.'

Yang Kwei Fei (*The Magnificent Concubine*).

5. The Film Makers

Extremely low production costs have repeatedly in boom times given Chinese film-making a 'licence to print money' tag. Costs, although higher now than a decade ago, are still stringent. Scriptwriters get roughly $1250 per movie, top directors $3000 and dubbers, who add the frenetic collage of shrieks and groans without which no action scene would be complete, some $250. Performers may be signed on for a year's trial, or given a five- to eight-year contract during which time they will be expected to make a minimum of four or five films per year. They are paid a monthly allowance, a bonus for each film made and an additional bonus for any film which has been exceptionally successful. It wasn't unusual in the old days for stars to be paid enormous sums on paper which they never saw in reality, or in the early 'sixties for a Shaws' starlet living in the studio dormitory block to be subsisting on a meagre dollar a day. Raymond Chow admits: 'I think it is true to say that in the past not many people in the film industry could have had a good life . . . not even after they had spent a good part of their life making movies.' A studio employee that I spoke to pointed out that, 'It is a very sad thing, everybody here is very badly paid.'

The Hong Kong industry is above all star-orientated. Shaws have always had a clearly voiced 'new faces' policy, something that ensures a steady flow of young, energetic and above all cheap talent into the studio. They have their own acting school to cope with the influx, in which tuition includes the martial arts and dance (originally offering a year's tuition, it is now a six-month course). Performers come from theatrical backgrounds – in Chinese opera, as in the case of Angela Mao, or they are child actors-cum-stuntmen, as David Chiang was, who began performing in films aged four, progressed to stunting, conjuring and swordfighting, before being given small fill-in parts, followed by a contract when he was eighteen. If would-be stars enter the company aged between fifteen and eighteen, chances are, while the men will be able to find roles to last them into their thirties, women will leave films altogether for marriage at 25; there are generally only small supporting roles for older women.

At Shaws, the female star will often have had her first contact with the company through a newspaper advertisement; or she may have been among the lucky ten out of three thousand at a giant audition. If that is the case, chances are she will have starred in six feature films, worked a sixteen-hour day, and been the subject of a couple of double-page spreads in the company's fan magazine eighteen months later.

Shih Szu in 1973 clinched her position as Shaws' topflight action star with an appearance in Hammer's *The Legend of the Seven Golden Vampires*. Having collected dancing trophies rapaciously as a child, Shih Szu at sixteen moved into Shaws' dormitory block with her mother, after winning a place at just such an audition. In her first film, *The Crimson Charm*, she was third on the cast list and died halfway through. In her second, she played the second lead – it was *Lady Hermit*, a much acclaimed and vastly commercial success, taking more than $165,500 in Hong Kong and in 1972 showing for a time in three Paris cinemas simul-

The Legend of the Seven Golden Vampires (1973/4): Shih Szu.

The Crimson Charm. (1969).

taneously. In *The Rescue* she was one of a group of Sung patriots rescuing a former Sung minister from prison. In *The Young Avenger* she played just that – training for ten years in the 'poisonous dragon' technique. In *Thunderbolt Fist* she was Red Butterfly, the martial arts instructress who implements revenge against Japan. In *Supermen Against the Orient*, a comic caper, she donned an old superman costume and rescued, with help, a pair of narcotics agents. When she started in 1969 she was often making three films simultaneously and snatching a few hours sleep on the set. Two years later she was down to two at a time. Now she makes fewer films – though she works without a break – and gets more money for the ones she does make.

Lady Hermit (1970): Shih Szu.

Lady Hermit.

The Young Avenger (1970): Shih Szu.

Thunderbolt Fist (1971).

Directors, too, are above all contract workers, whose fate is dependent on the take their latest film has managed to gross. The careers of a handful of the current top money-making Hong Kong directors cuts a fairly wide swathe through the history of the last few decades of Chinese film. Huang Feng (*Hap Ki Do* and *Stoner*) started with Shaws after coming out of the army after the war. At Shaws he worked his way stolidly from grip to assistant cameraman, to assistant director and director. In 1970 he completed his contract with them and went to work for Golden Harvest where he has concentrated on action films. Lo Wei, responsible for the first Bruce Lee films,

Lo Wei.

started acting at sixteen in North China (he is in his fifties) with touring theatrical troupes. During the Japanese invasions he continued touring with groups, putting on patriotic plays. He went to Shanghai and became a star there at a time when Shanghai was known as the Hollywood of China, moving to Hong Kong in 1948. Working first as an actor he turned to directing with Cathay before moving to Shaws, where he completed his contract with films like *Vengeance of a Snow*

Girl in 1970 and the atmospheric *Dragon Swamp*. Some months of independent film-making followed – there was a project called *The Lovely Female Fighter* – before he became Golden Harvest's foremost action director.

Chu Yuan made *The Killer* (*The Sacred Knights of Vengeance*) in 1971 and *Intimate Confessions of a Chinese Courtesan* the same year. Educated in China, he came to Hong Kong in 1955, became an assistant director at 21 and director at 23. In 1960 he made an essay in social realism that was shown widely in China as well as in Europe, about the plight of a Hong Kong family. In 1968, when the Cantonese industry collapsed – 'too much was being made too fast' – he joined Cathay, then the second largest film studio in Hong Kong, where he made *The Cassette Killer*, a thriller. He finished his contract with four more thrillers and moved to Shaws, where he has faced such archetypal studio tasks as making the film to rebuild a dying star's reputation and getting rather reluctantly swept up in the kung fu craze. He is almost satisfied with *Intimate Confessions* 'apart from the kung fu scenes . . . but the boss said, we must have kung fu . . it was still possible to sell a film on kung fu then . . . so we had kung fu. The boss makes kung fu films for money. The director makes them because he has to eat. The audience goes to the first, the second, the third for the excitement. The fourth? They don't go to the fourth. It has been too easy . . . all those companies shooting films in two days, a week. There are two hundred martial arts schools in Hong Kong. You can pick up someone . . . anyone, just like that. They won't be Bruce Lee, or Lo Lieh, it will just be kung fu and probably fake kung fu at that.'

Chu Yuan has just signed a new contract with Shaws that stipulates four films a year. 'Two or three are still possible . . . four is simply too much.'

Intimate Confessions of a Chinese Courtesan (1971).

He is currently working on his tenth film for the company; his earlier ones include *Duel for Gold*, *The Couples* and *The Bastard*. He has a soft spot for the latter which he wrote himself from an idea by a retired Shaws script writer – it is an exposé of a corrupt big businessman. His latest two films – *Hong Kong '73* and *Seventy-two Tenants* – mark a return to the more social concerns he prefers.

Women are noticeably absent at direction level in both studios, and they are rare at production level (although Shaws does have at least one woman executive). There do, though, seem to be a number of women both producing and directing independently in the action field. Ex-film critic Li Yin recently completed *Left Hand of Death*, a kung fu film about a farmer who just

happens to be a martial arts expert; and the latest film by Tung Yuet Juwen, an established director, is *Buffalo Hsiung* in which the two lead roles are taken by boxers.

Going independent seems from the outside a logical alternative to the tight restrictions of studio work, and a number of actors and directors have opted for just this alternative – Lee, of course, Wang Yu, the excellent King Hu, who also put in formative years with Shaws (he worked as assistant director on *Eternal Love* in the early 'sixties), but it is far from being an accessible alternative to those without either a string of major financial successes or a private income. Chu Yuan, for instance, saw little prospect of himself moving in that direction. Nor did Angela Mao.

Intimate Confessions of a Chinese Courtesan.

6. Kung Fu Chronology

In the mid-sixties Shaws made good their ambition of bringing all the technical proficiency money could buy to Chinese films. The technically superior films that resulted were shot in Mandarin on budgets that could range from as much as $200,000 to some two million (for *The Goddess of Mercy* in 1966). However, alongside these, until the bottom dropped out of the market a couple of years later, Shaws continued to turn out those cheap Cantonese films at the rate of eighty to a hundred a year, on something like a week's schedule each. The closest comparison as far as western film-making goes is probably with the American studios of the 'thirties and 'forties, a time when even a small studio like RKO could turn out some dozen or so Tim Holt Westerns or maybe a handful of low budget series like *The Saint* alongside its more prestigious efforts each year.

The One-armed Swordsman (1968) may mark the return to popularity of the Chinese swordplay film, but its true origin lies in the 'twenties. Toward the end of that decade, the classic Chinese subjects that had been enormously successful with a public constantly regaled with Western-style films made against token Chinese backgrounds were overtaken by a wave of Chinese 'westerns'. Jay Leyda describes them in *Dianying* in terms which sound very familiar to any one who has sampled the second generation swordplay film, 'the central figure (usually male) was placed in some undefined period – he was a synthesis of medieval knight errant, Japanese samurai, French Fantomas and Robin Hood . . . his or her death-defying exploits were prolonged

without any discipline other than "entertainment".' They were almost continuous bursts of swordplay laced with intervals for romance or sex. The hero's or heroine's antagonists could be rich or evil, demons or ghosts. At the beginning of the 'thirties some two hundred swordplay films were made and they were all vastly successful. They can also lay claim, as Jay Leyda points out, to being the most escapist films in China's entire history. And their basis was less in literature than in current adventure serials and newspaper comic strips. Within a few years, however, Robin Hood had come out of his temporal limbo and turned patriot in a series of patriotic anti-Japanese films. Then even that last avenue to the present was closed through the imposition of a rigorous censorship code that for a time even forbade all mention of the Japanese in films. (Censorship in fact still plays a large part in the policy of all film makers in Hong Kong but perhaps most heavily at Shaws. Anything seriously controversial is avoided, although they are willing to test their audience's tolerance on matters like sex and violence. Partly, too, the situation is encouraged by the nitpicking censorship regulations observed in the South-east Asian countries in which the films are distributed. Perhaps censorship also, along with heavy contract clauses, produces the curiously contentless feeling that dogs many of their costume films and which, as the 'fistplay' films usurped the conventional sword movie, seem often to have drained these costume dramas even of their latent themes of knightly amity and heroism.)

Mad About Music (1963).

Operation Macao (1966).

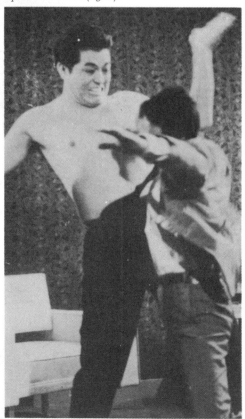

If the early 'sixties were some kind of a beginning of a major boom for the Hong Kong-based Chinese film industry, it was a boom kept for a time within parochial limits by the kinds of films involved: musicals, romances, social dramas with titles like *Tea Time Chatter, Mad About Music,* and *Passion* – films that did not hesitate to cash in on more than just the titles of already-popular Western films. Hence the current top action director Lo Wei was to be found kicking his heels around a project called *An Affair to Remember* which he made for Cathay in 1963.

Between 1960 and 1968 an unbelievable thirty new cinemas opened in Hong Kong alone. Along with a steady stream of Western films, a small flood of Toho science-fiction movies were imported to feed the hungry audience, along with Toshiro Mifune's latest sword films. The Hong Kong film industry began to regale its public with an endless stream of pseudo-James Bond exercises – Bond parodies, carbon copies, interpretations. . . . By 1966 a favourite fan magazine ploy was a spread of the latest new star in a series of judo poses. And then Cathay announced the logical result of carefully hedged bets – a singing swordfight heroine. At the same time they even went so far as to announce that Betty Loh Ti, the subject of regular spreads in their magazine, was taking up kung fu for her part in *Travel with a Sword,* while Yoong Yoong, who has long since dropped completely from the public eye, was declared Asia's 'number one martial arts star'. The genre had obviously arrived.

In 1962 Shaws had made a film called *The Last Woman of Shang* for some $800,000. It was a superbly atmospheric piece set in China's feudal past, brilliantly shot and lit. The scenes of conflict took back seat to the gradual unfolding of the rest of the

James Bond Chinese Style (1967).

action. And if in *Come Drink with Me* made in 1965, the fight scenes were again part of a mosaic of intrigue built around gradually registered happenings in an inn, by 1968 the sword hero had definitively returned with Wang Yu and *The One-armed Swordsman*.

Shaws' lavish productions had taken great pains to reproduce on screen every smallest elaboration of on-set detail. Sets were festooned with hangings, thick with intricate carvings, gleaming with gold – detail was piled on detail in an attempt to recreate the magnificence of China's dynastic past. Never a shadow was allowed to obscure the

The Last Woman of Shang (1962).

Come Drink With Me (1965).

·magnificence. The effect in colour on the screen was dazzling and it is still extraordinary to see such essays in sheer weighty magnificence in one of Kowloon's run-down, poorer cinemas. It was all about as far away from the soot and whitewash effect of the black and white Cantonese quickies as can be imagined. The stories oscillated around dynastic rivalries, favourite concubines, scheming rulers, clandestine meetings, elaborate plots involving cross-dressing, disguise and the inevitable love of Emperor for country girl.

As the action film came into its own, Shaws may have borrowed from Japanese sword-play films, but they also quite perceptibly met it half-way by adapting their house style. For instance, the grandiose setting for the Empress Wu in the film of the same name transformed itself without too much effort into the panorama of death that is all that is left of the dungeons of Tiger Fort after the avenger has achieved his goal. And the Empress herself (played by Li Li-hua), dressed in white, becomes more or less reincarnated in the figure of Wang Yu as the death-dealing hero in the later film. The visual ornateness that appeared in those adaptations of ancient Chinese myths and fables, reworkings of operas and so on, as a weighty elaboration of the set itself, appears at first in the action films as an equally ornate and painstaking choreography of violence, before the conflict itself is pared down to a series of one-to-one contests of strength and skill, where the only ornateness lies in the way move and counter-move are instrumented within the space of the screen.

Chinese action films repeatedly turn on a handful of recognizable visual motifs: the stricken man or woman, cornered or dying (*The Rivals*, 1968); the exotic villain representing marauding Mongolian hordes, as in *The Bandits of Shantung* (1971); or in the elaborately regarded costume of the professional

Golden Swallow (1969): Wang Yu.

The Rivals (1968).

Bandits from Shantung (1971).

The Killer (1971).

Japanese karate fighter, whose deliberate stepping down from his high stilted shoes signals, quite as resonantly as the equally deliberate presentation of the hero's 'special weapon' in the martial arts school films, that a new depth of conflict is about to begin.

Film after film specifically relishes the mystery of the struggle. Owing something to the core of transcendentalism at the heart of arts like *tai chi* in which the sign of a complete master is the ability to perform almost supernatural acts, the fight is glorified through such embellishments as impossible leaps, sequences in which the hero or heroine simply takes to the air, walks on treetops (*Zatoichi and the One-armed Swordsman*, 1970), or on water (*The Invincible Eight*, 1970), who catches flying arrows in mid-air or a swordblade in mid-blow. (*Deadly Duo*, 1971, or *The Blade Spares None*, 1969–70).

In the swordplay films the scenes of conflict are there to decorate the codes of knighthood and heroism that are the subjects of these elaborate artifices which embrace virtues like reverence to elders, personal honour and unwavering devotion to the cause. One of the most striking contrasts between the swordplay film and the kung fu film is in the area of relationships. Both are plagued with the 'idealized' image of romantic love in which the woman is confined to the edges of the plot for long stretches of the film, only emerging at the end to weep over her hero's body or celebrate his victory. But the swordplay film can go beyond this to allow its female characters a welcome freedom of movement, independence and a central role in the action. At the end of the film she may stay with a fellow knight who has crossed her path, or simply take to the road, as she does at the end of *Lady Hermit* (1969) for instance. The swordswomen of the extensive series of costume films are some of the most charismatic

Lady Hermit (1969): Cheng Pei-Pei.

figures that the Chinese cinema has revealed. For this, much praise should go to the actresses: Cheng Pei Pei, in *Lady Hermit* and *Come Drink with Me* (1965); Shih Szu as the lady of the law, in the film of the same name, who lures two rival robber bands to an inn so she can annihilate both of them; Nora Miao Ker-Hsiu in *The Invincible Eight;* or the icily evocative Hsu Feng in *The Fate of Lee Khan* (1973).

The Blade Spares None (1969–70) is a very formal and theatrical enterprise and one differentiated from the run of the mill by its quiet humour and remarkably fine direction by Yen Tung-Chu. Its plot is based on the exposure of a mysterious prince who lures first-rate fighters into his service, selecting them through a gruelling test, after which they are never heard of again. There are any number of superbly rendered sequences – an adolescent boy running in his nightclothes through empty streets, a bloody sword in one hand, to an open air feast that he finds strangely silent – the guests lie dead around the table; or the opening con-

Come Drink With Me (1965).

test of skill fought on a circular platform raised high above the ground; or the scenes in which the swordswoman, played with great elegance by Nora Miao Ker-Hsiu, unmasks (literally) the prince and leads two brother swordsmen in a raid on his underground treasure store. The whole is enlivened by some fine touches of humour as the rivalry develops between the two swordsmen. This gives their relationship and that between them and the swordswoman a kind of gentle reciprocality not found in, for instance, those romantic interludes with ever-faithful loved ones. In *The Hurricane* (directed by Lo Wei in 1970), Nora Miao was again teamed with Hsieh Hsien combating pro-Mongolian traitors in the Sung Dynasty, and at the end of that year, in *The Comet Strikes*, the same team confronted a supposedly haunted mansion which they found to contain more solid adversaries than ghosts.

The Invincible Eight (1970).

The Fate of Lee Khan (1973): Hsu Feng.

Lady of the Law (1969).

As the 'sixties drew to a close, a drift became noticeable away from the traditional swordplay film and towards films in which the actual fight, the contest itself, became so increasingly important that it finally took over the whole film. About this time, Golden Harvest moved into the studios of the now defunct production wing of Cathay (they satisfied themselves with the less risky field of distribution). And the stage was set for the steady stream of kung fu films that drew an audience on a world scale. Golden Harvest made *Stormy Sun* (*Superman Chu*) in 1970, *The Big Boss* with Bruce Lee in 1971. Shaws made *The Killer* and *King Boxer* (*Five Fingers of Death*) the same year; other sure-fire successes followed, along with a flood of independent quickies shot anywhere within the South-east Asia ambience, such as *End of the Wicked Tiger*, *Inheritor of Kung Fu* (made by the aptly named Goldig Productions) and *A Tooth for a Tooth*. In 1973,

King Boxer surprised observers by climbing the hallowed ground of *Variety's* top grossers list . . . There was nothing else to be done but for even the most prestigious companies to follow suit.

The martial arts became the subject of the film, and the ultimate deterrent the human weapon. The elaborate weaponry of the period films was cast aside, and the physical contest became quite specifically that of the world of martial arts schools and tournaments. In *Hap ki Do* Angela Mao pared the wandering swordswoman heroine down to a core of asceticism and determination. Her movements are more circumscribed than her predecessors' because her world is too. It is tighter, more classical, less romantic. If she is still the repository of purity and self-denial it is a purity based less on the freewheeling romanticism of the characters she creates in her other films, and more on the rigorous pursuance of a series of spelt out rules. The hero or heroine is

The Chinese Boxer (1970): Wang Yu

Hap Ki Do (1971): Angela Mao.

given a surrogate family, a band of fellow workers, as in *The Big Boss* or, more usually, of fellow classmates at the martial arts school with the revered teacher at their head. Often as not, it is also an environment in which it is easy to mix themes of personal and national destiny: the aggressive unruly 'false' school functions as a straightforward stand-in for the institutions involved in Japanese imperialism or for their less overt infiltration into Chinese life.

The scenario is familiar. Establishing shot of exterior of school plus the much revered almost talismanic sign over the entrance. Cut to interior and a panorama of working-out bodies. From this point, events escalate in a direct progression; from the first aphorism from the revered teacher to the first hint of his knowledge of a particular arcane technique never to be used in anger for purely personal reasons; then to the act of deliberate provocation from a rival establishment whose operations may be a simple front for nefarious dealings in

Hap Ki Do.

arms or drugs; then to a series of fights of increasing fierceness.

Film after film will hang on the use of a special technique invested with more or less arcane significance – we may even, as in *Lady Whirlwind*, see the ancient sage hand over the treasured volume and hear him intone the instructions to the novice hero. The *tai chi* 'iron palm', or 'fist' or 'hand' as it is also called, becomes, as the reward for much pain and perseverance, the instrument of revenge in *The One-armed Boxer*, *The Chinese Boxer*, *King Boxer* and *The Manchu Boxer*. The 'invisible kick' embellishes *The Master of Kung Fu*, a film made around events in the life of the famous Cantonese boxer Huang Fei Hung. Elsewhere the screen is alive with 'iron claws', or 'head-crushers' (*Kung Fu the Headcrusher*), and of course, nothing if not literal minded, *Enter the Dragon* actually awards its Fu Manchu-style villain an artificial hand actually constructed from steel knife-blades.

Hap Ki Do.

Chinese Boxer (1969/70): Wang Yu.

A particular style of martial art can be imbued with equally pervasive overtones: the Korean art of *taek-wondo* in *When Taekwondo Strikes* or *Tiger of the Northland; shaolin boxing* in *The Shaolin Boxer* and the television series *Kung Fu*, *hap ki do* in the Angela Mao film of the same name, as can a particular weapon, as we saw above with the lethal *nanchaku*, and also three or four sectional staffs (*New One-armed Swordsman*, for instance) or even whips (in *Whiplash*).

The studio sets in films built around rival martial arts school conflicts function simply as an arena; we provide the audience and the performers provide the physical action that has to be enthralling enough to keep us involved for two hours or more, whether they are simply picking off lesser fighters or cornering the supreme master in a fight to the death.

The once-knightly-heroic rambling narrative becomes a peg for the construction of a series of revenge-motivated tournaments that in turn become increasingly 'real' from film to film. This culminates in Bruce Lee's obsessive feeding back into film of every last detail of his physical prowess in the most flamboyant way possible, complete with a repertoire of the world's top martial artists to fight against.

As the fantasy film evolves towards full-blown tournament there are still one or two stops along the way. One is Wang Yu's *One-armed Boxer*, a spectacular example of the omnibus approach to the tournament film. Wang Yu equipped with the iron-hand technique and the *tai chi* death grip which can stop circulation at a particularly deadly point in the body ('two inches down from the shoulder and one along') confronts in turn two Thai boxers, a judo expert, a karate master, a *taek-wondo* exponent, an Indian yoga and a pair of Tibetan lamas. Wang Yu was to go on, in *Seaman Number Seven* (*Wang*

Yu's Seven Magnificent Fights, 1972), to prove he could also play through a virtually continuous fight and maintain all the tension expected of an expertly written thriller.

Revenge within the context of the martial arts establishments is a common enough theme and highly ritualistic, with its emphasis on codes of loyalty and the redeeming of insults to teacher or fellow pupils, which escalates towards the rooting-out of what sometimes seems more like an arbitrary evil than a specific enemy. But neither the revenge itself nor the martial arts are always framed in such a relatively pure context.

Back-alley fights erupt in service areas, in the uninspiring tenements of Hong Kong's lower income groups, on the back of stationary trucks, in dark unfrequented streets. And revenge is often enough a metaphor of sorts for social action. An interesting point here is that, at one point in the chequered career of the kung fu movie, these martial arts films were being produced in Hong Kong by a Communist Chinese-owned production company, which then distributed the results through their own cinemas. According to report they were stylistically identical with the commercial product, it was just that the impetus to revolt came through loud and clear.

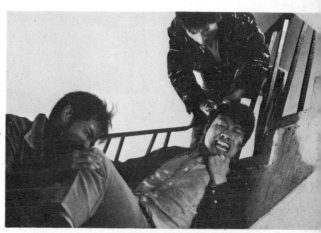

Payment in Blood (1972): Yueh Hua.

Payment in Blood (1972) is revealing, despite its misjudged if worthy attempt to show proper respect for human feelings through resort to the unalloyed and highly predictable ploys of melodrama. The film manages to end up confirming a position in no uncertain terms in which the individual is shown to be powerless against organized crime, and his supposed defenders, the police, equally ineffectual. It locates the gang head, for once not the other side of some exotic robe but quite tangibly in the executive suite of a Hong Kong stock company with his

Payment in Blood: Yueh Hua.

name on the door. It even goes so far as to bring the final bloody combat right onto the floor of the stock exchange, mingling blood and money and industrial speculation in a single bold sequence. The fights are a grimy business, following the bewildered witness to a murder, from home to workplace and back, in the context of crowded and polluted over-spill areas of Hong Kong.

In *The Greatest Thai Boxing* (1973), a modestly budgeted effort, the boxing ring itself becomes just one arena out of many in which money purchases sufficient muscle power to keep those that have it suspended a safe distance from the gutter, if not in the lap of luxury. *The Greatest Thai Boxing* was made by an independent company that seems to consist basically of the same group who made *Kung Fu the Head-crusher*, in which an undercover cop smashes a smuggling ring, and *King of Kung Fu*, a more diffuse effort but one

that manages some spirited fights in the name of revenge.

The social aspect of the back-alley style fight film isn't always shown with such blackness. In 1972 director Lo Wei came up with a film that by rights should have been a disaster. It was called *Back Alley Princess* and was a socially conscious comedy that inevitably managed to signal its gags a little too heavily. However, while supposedly charting the more or less careless lives of two street kids (one of whom just happens to be a girl dressed as a boy), the film was able to sketch in, without too much over-emphasis, life in an over-crowded Hong Kong on the brink of desperation – the protection racket that decimates the earnings of small stall-holders, the casual glimpses into the unglamorised world of bar hostesses and prostitution, and around them a persuasive array of small-time gamblers, pimps and general hustlers. Even the fairy godmother figure – in the

Back Alley Princess (1972).

shape of a do-good lawyer – isn't
totally an escapist figure. It is casually
revealed that he not only lives in a
vast mansion in unabashed luxury, but
he lives there alone – a thing unheard
of in the packed-out tenements half-a-
mile away. To any one who has seen
The Big Boss the final fight on the lawn
will ring familiar – only this goes one
better: here the boss is destroyed by
twin simultaneous flying kicks to the
head administered by the twin heroines
of the film.

'Death to the enemy' is a frequent
war cry – sometimes actually articulated, sometimes just made plain
through the course of the action. The
enemy comes to Chinese action films
in nothing if not rococo form: stilted
Japanese warriors, sword experts in
outlandish costumes, enormous muscled
monsters with shaven heads and boorish
manners, fanged karate experts . . . and
always behind the warriors the real
villains, the big bosses who run the

Master of Kung Fu (1972).

smuggling outfits, who plan invasions on a hot line to Tokyo, who liaise with Europeans who have a finger in the opium trade and a pernicious need to feast on hack killing routines dressed up as martial arts tournaments. In *The Master of Kung Fu* the European businessman shouts 'Kill! Kill!' from his front row seat at a crooked tournament, never noticing that that is exactly what is happening in the ring and that the fight is rigged – the villain has metal blocks strapped to his elbows under his costume.

As much a staple figure as the Boss and his musclemen is the inevitable go-between. The best of this line must be the unnamed actor in *The Greatest Thai Boxing*: an androgynous Bette Davis-style seven-stone weakling, who wears his loud print shirt hanging over his trousers and spends his time fussily combing and recombing his suitably dank locks, or the sly, hatted hanger-on in *Hap ki Do*.

Master of Kung Fu.

The villains are noticeably the ones who have the power, whether it is in a kung fu quickie shot in two days on a beach in Taiwan, or an elaborate swordplay film that brings into play the whole heavy repertoire of Shaws' massive sets. They can be twisted rulers, scheming rival feudal lords, gangsters. . . . At best the hero or heroine will find himself or herself confronted by an enemy bent on increasing his territory, or will find himself accidentally forced into collision with a power structure that has been there all along but which he has never noticed. Almost inevitably, too, the potential social statement tends to get lost in the melodrama and fist-waving, or subsumed in the often-repeated message about attacks on the national interest made by the Japanese. So the man with the silk clothes, the ivory cigarette holder, the paid-for women with their westernized looks and the unpleasant sexual proclivities, who may or may not himself be a fighter but who nonetheless has the town in his pocket, becomes a symbol for everything that is to be resisted, and wanders almost unchanged from film to film. He may be the blatant street fighter of *The Greatest Thai Boxing*, or the dyed blonde Japanese of *Seaman Number Seven* who has a continual round of sumo wrestling played out in the airy, luxury mansion for his amusement, or the aesthete turned gangster, or the martial arts master who puts his art to evil use.

Taking the image of the Chinese in western films and superimposing it on the image of the often Japanese enemy in Chinese films, the two seem to all but coincide. Chinese films can be as xenophobic as any produced in the West – and with more reason. And they allow, of course, for appearances sometimes being deceptive: the shaven-headed warrior in *King Boxer* who is shocked by the callousness of the gang who have hired him and who quits, almost taking all interest in the film with him as he is the most suggestive and involving character.

Because the conflict has to be fought out at a physical level involving skill, the opponent, however unpleasant his leanings, will still have to be able to provide the hero or heroine with an opportunity to do more than wipe the floor with him . . . something that keeps the films, for all their eye-gouging, groin-kicking and elegant fountains of blood, this side of close-up sadism.

King Boxer (1971).

THE BAMBOO HOUSE OF DOLLS
導演
桂治洪
羅烈
碧蒂杜芙
領銜主演
PRODUCER
DIRECTED BY
STARRING
BIRTE TOVE
LO LIEH
王俠
劉慧茹
妮姬蕙
羅夏英
李海淑
高尚美
主演
樊梅生
詹森
李敏郎
高雄
陳鳳鎮
合演
女集中營
SB
A CHINESE PICTURE WITH ENGLISH SUBTITLES
邵氏兄弟(香港)有限公司出品全部彩色

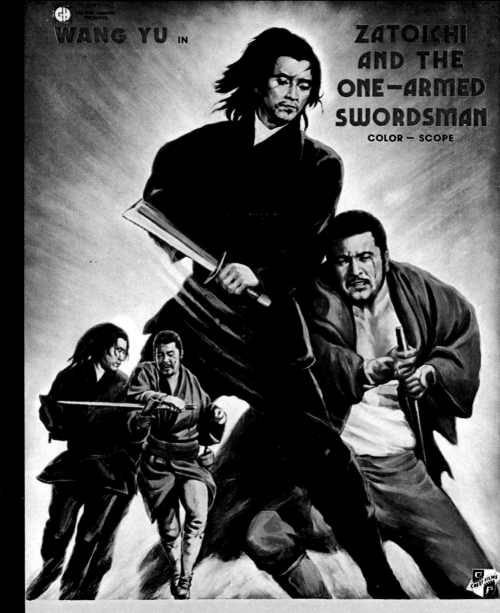

8.Lady Kung Fu: Angela Mao

'Is she that fierce?'
'Yes.'
'What is her background?'
'I don't know, but she came looking for Ling Shi-hau.'
'Uhhhhh!'
Lady Whirlwind/Deep Thrust

In *Hap Ki Do* (*Lady Kung Fu*) Angela Mao demonstrates a dazzling array of kicks, blocks and neck-crushing foot grips in a series of directly aggressive and angry onslaughts. She has been playing fighting roles since she was five – first in Chinese opera and then in film. Characteristically in performance, she approaches her roles seriously, directly and without a trace of narcissism.

The Invincible Eight (1970): Nora Miao Ker-hsiu and Angela Mao.

It was an Angela Mao film that was the first Golden Harvest film after the Lee bonanza to attain wide release. It came at a time when it was automatically assumed that her films, *Hap Ki Do* (1970) especially, but also *Lady Whirlwind* (*Deep Thrust*, 1971), were an exotic response to the growing influence of the Women's Liberation Movement that had provided Hollywood with the means to ring the changes on their 'black' films. There, the final touch, in *Cleopatra Jones*, was to make the central character not only a fighter – deft mastery of a few elementary karate routines soon accomplished that – and black, but also a woman and the employee of the United States Government. *Hap Ki Do* however had less to do with *Cleopatra Jones* than with the preceding generation of swordfight heroines and with the fighting roles that are found alongside acrobatic ones in Chinese opera. Having a woman in the central role doesn't really change anything in the films in terms of motivation, and they are situated as much as ever either in the distant past, during the Japanese occupation, and (more rarely) in the organized crime-dominated world of the back-street present.

When she was nineteen, Angela Mao signed her current five-year contract with Golden Harvest. It was 1970, and that year she made the first of four films she was to complete that year, *Angry River*, a film that was directed by Huang Feng who, with Lo Wei, was to become one of her two regular directors.

It opens with a montage of inexplicable slaughter as a bride arrives dead at a wedding, two horsemen collapse dead

Angry River (1970).

from their horses, and Angela Mao as the daughter of a famous martial arts master finds her father struck down, though not dead. To save him she goes in search of the antidote – the Black Herb – and the film documents her quest as she overcomes the supernatural trials that are placed in her path. The film relishes the dichotomy between power and powerlessness that forms the core of the 'One-armed' series with the heroine spending part of her time as a normally skilled martial artist, part – for this is the cost of obtaining the herb – stripped of her powers and reliant on her own wit and the combined muscle and goodwill of the men around her, and the final third burning with superhuman strength that is made completely explicit on the screen (she actually glows). Her first hazard is an attack by the green-clad Lunar Sect which she demolishes – leaving the camera to pan philosophically over an array of body-festooned trees; the second, the river itself which bursts into flames when tested by shooting an arrow into it; the third, a series of confrontations with the Giant who guards the ancient bearded figure of the Merciless One, who (literally) flies to the rescue impressed by the strength of her 'filial loyalty'. The film is replete with wild landscapes, flying figures and even brings out its own Toho-like monster. Half-witted though the tale may be, it summons all its waning energy in the last reel for an impressive confrontation between the leader of the Lunar Sect who arrives with suitable ostentation, equipped with a gold claw on a stick and a suitably unearthly laugh, and our superhuman heroine.

In *The Invincible Eight* (1970) the theme is again one of revenge taken on the perpetrators of evil against the family. In this case, the eight are all sons and daughters of those who have been murdered in the cause of personal advancement by one General Hsiao – against advice he spared the eight, then still children. They come together, drawn magnetically to the same target, and decide to unite their efforts. Interestingly, the character Angela Mao plays in this film – the warrior woman dressed as a man carrying a fan which conceals a lethal weapon – is placed against that evoked by Nora Miao Ker-hsiu as the archetypal female good spirit whose powers – lethal strength and skill allied to the use of the faster-than-the-human-eye darts – are hidden behind a veneer of total submissiveness.

(The film came at a point when there was a campaign to make Nora Miao a star, since when her career seems to have run aground on the back-up parts she took in the Bruce Lee films.) Director Lo Wei, always happier grinding out the action than sustaining tension between various episodes or personalities, invokes a whole museum of Chinese weaponry, including primitive hand grenades, double axes and a fiendishly clever extemporized scissor weapon for coping with the whip troupe. In an outrageous climax, the General battles on regardless, despite having accumulated some half dozen knives in his back and stomach and a cleaver in the chest – he brings about his own end by toppling on to his back, thereby ramming all the knives home simultaneously.

The Invincible Eight.

Lady Whirlwind (1971): Angela Mao.

Lady Whirlwind.

If 'filial loyalty' launched these two heroines on their respective paths towards revenge, in *Lady Whirlwind* (*Deep Thrust*) it is loyalty to a sister. Tien (Angela Mao) arrives in town searching for the man who abandoned her sister after making her pregnant, causing her to take her own life. But the film is based in fact around a double revenge tale, for while Tien seeks Ling Shih-hua, he has been in hiding for three years improving his fight technique so that he can finally break the power of the leader of the opium and gambling syndicate who once attempted to take his life. It is also the only revenge film I have come across in which revenge is finally waived, by Tien of course, out of deference to the fact that Ling has eliminated the gang, or out of respect for the woman who has been caring for him all these years, perhaps?

There are some excellent early sequences, notably one in which Angela Mao goes through the whole routine of the Western hero's portentous stroll into a bar room in territory that we sense is not his own. Only here it is a gambling hall crammed with men, into which she laconically strolls – leaving the bank broken and the croupier cowering under the table.

The Fate of Lee Khan (1970–73) took three years to complete. The director, King Hu, who also made *Come Drink with Me* is a notable historian, lecturer and inventor of the first Chinese teletype. He is renowned for the accuracy of his historical reconstructions and, as he himself puts it, he 'allows his characters to fight with many other weapons than just fists and swords'. Set during the Yuan dynasty, a time when the people were rising against Mongol rule, the film deals with Lee Khan's plot to get hold of the revolutionaries' war map – an act complicated by the existence of

traitors on both sides, and by the wiles of a revolutionary group at whose centre is Wendy (Li Li-hua), the owner of the Spring Inn. She sends out the word and gathers around her four colleagues from previous campaigns, whom she disguises as waitresses – an opportunity for some neat by-play between them and their contentious customers as they settle down to wait for events to unfold. It is not that the fights are any less complex than in the more blatant fight films, it is just that they take on a new power through the carefully registered tale of intrigue that

The Fate of Lee Khan (1970/73): Angela Mao and Hsiu Feng.

forms their context, a tale laced with humour and much shrewd observation, all of which gives the final heroic tussle on a deserted beach an almost Homeric scope. Angela Mao appears as one of the revolutionaries, the one who survives to the end to combat Lee Khan face to face and to kill him before dying herself. She has never performed better in an impressive production and one that incidentally offers a superb rebuttal to all those films that leave their heroines languishing in the wings. The clear-eyed revolutionary women are vigorously at the centre of things.

The Fate of Lee Khan.

Hap Ki Do was made in the same year as *Fist of Fury* and it is the only film she has made to date in the 'rival schools' format. Angela Mao plays one of three leading martial arts exponents expelled from Korea for openly resisting Japanese aggression (it is 1934 and Korea is under Japanese occupation). They are instructed by their teachers to return to China and set up a martial arts school there, passing on their knowledge of *hap ki do* to others. However, their first polite attempt to pay their respects to the neighbouring Black Bear school ends in a small-scale war. It is no accident that the Black Bear school is Japanese. *Hap Ki Do* contains probably as much fight

footage as it is possible to cram into this particular kind of film and, in spite of disappointingly flat direction from Huang Feng, and the fact that it ultimately stops short of allowing Angela Mao a position of power equal to that of Bruce Lee in *Fist of Fury*, it does at least give her a more satisfactory window for her skills than her next film *Enter the Dragon*.

In that film she appears as Bruce Lee's sister in a flashback, pursued by gang, fighting back, but ultimately recognizing that there are more than she can handle and stabbing herself with a handy sliver of glass. It is a curious scene in which the suicide is at odds

Enter the Dragon (1973).

Hap Ki Do (1971).

with the whole conception of the fight hero or heroine in Chinese films – everyone knows he or she would have gone down fighting. Later that year she played a Chinese girl sent to aid the patriots in *When Taekwondo Strikes*, a film again set in Korea under Japanese occupation but boasting one novel ingredient – a female European *taekwondo* expert who plays the niece of the Catholic priest from whose church the *taekwondo* Grand Master and super-patriot operates. In *Stoner – the Shrine of Ultimate Bliss* again directed by Huang Feng, Angela Mao, incarnating her familiar fight heroine, joins forces with law-and-order narcotics

man, played by George Lazenby, to smash a false temple that is dedicated to hooking its converts on something more solidly addictive than religion.

Angela Mao also has roles in *Thunderbolt* (1970) a film based, like Shaws' *Thunderbolt Fist* (1971), around the acquisition of a new fighting skill; and in *Back Alley Princess*. In the latter film she gives one of her most sympathetic performances as one of the medicine show performers, the one who, with Shang Kuan Ling Fung as the 'Princess' of the title, personally leads an onslaught on the garish mansion of the vice-king, an onslaught which starts in his poster-decorated bedroom and ends on the lawn outside.

When Taekwondo Strikes (1973).

Back Alley Princess (1972).
Enter the Dragon: Angela Mao and attacker.

Opium Trail (Deadly China Doll) (1973).

9. The Dance of Death: Bruce Lee

'Bruce Lee and his Singing Rod of Death . . . Bruce Lee is the real superstar!'
Trailer for *Fist of Fury*

In 1971 Bruce Lee's first film was released in Hong Kong. Superficially it wasn't all that different from the hundreds of other low-budget action films that were made that year in Thailand, Taiwan, Korea or Hong Kong, but unlike the others, it was not just successful but broke box office records wherever it showed, out-taking films like *The Sound of Music*. The follow-up was an even greater success. Ticket touts were charging £15 a ticket in Singapore where half a million people saw the film. It was 1972 and despite the films being shown at the Cannes film festival that year, little of this escaped beyond the mandarin circuit . . . even though there was the same story of packed houses and near riots at Cannes. The following year, both films had broken decisively into the world market. And by July, Bruce Lee, a star at thirty, was dead, aged thirty-two, in mysterious circumstances that not even an inquest finally clarified, that gave his story all the makings of a personal myth and that sparked off a death cult of James Dean or Buddy Holly proportions.

A huge commemorative poster of him went up in Hong Kong and thousands packed the streets outside the funeral parlour. Lee Marvin, Steve McQueen and James Garner were among his pall bearers. The press invoked the scenes at Valentino's death. There were rumours that Lee, who had been found in a coma, had died of an overdose – the resemblance to the deaths of those other cult figures, Janis Joplin and Jimi Hendrix, was too close not to be noticed – or that the overdose had been of a body-building drug – that his quest for physical perfection finally caught up with him. There were other rumours: that he had been the object of an attack that for once materialized out of one of the many crank threats that he received; that he had been assassinated by a rival business faction; that he was in some Hong Kong mafia deal and had tried to get out; and last, that he was not really dead at all, but he had staged the whole thing and gone into hiding. Lee's wife was driven to make a statement to the press affirming that she 'held no one person or group of persons responsible' for his death. But she couldn't stop the speculation. And somewhere between Hong Kong and Seattle, where his body was taken for burial, his $200,000 coffin was 'damaged in transit' so badly that his body had to be displayed in a new one.

Bruce Lee.

Essentially the legend was based on three films. *The Big Boss* (1971) was Lee's first film. It can still lay claim to being his best, both from the point of view of its scenes of street-fighting heroism and of the very straightforward way the plot, about the hick country boy who confronts the gangland head – and wins, unfolds. Lee plays the new boy at the ice factory who is perplexed by the disappearance of his work-mates. He discovers that the boss is using the factory as a front for his big time heroin smuggling activities. Avoiding the hired killers and the smoother bait that is laid in his path, he single-handedly decimates the gang and destroys its leader. Confronted at one point by twenty gang members all armed with knives, chains and sticks he carefully demolishes each of them in turn, concluding by kicking their knives back into their own bodies and following through with a graphically clear thrust to the rib cage. The film offers some nicely judged contrasts between the opulence of the boss's household, a lavish bungalow complete with retinue of Westernised women, servants and a wayward gangster son, and the unpretentiousness of the workers' collective household.

In *Fist of Fury* (1972) Lee plays a member of a martial arts school who revolts body and soul against the anti-Chinese prejudice rife at the time (it is set in Shanghai in 1938, a time of Japanese encroachment and civil war). On one level, the film is a fraught revenge tragedy with Lee plunging into his teacher's grave and scraping the earth off the coffin in a paroxysm of anger and grief, on another a straight forward rival martial arts school epic. Lee (as Chen) suspects that his teacher has been poisoned by a rival Japanese school. He confirms these suspicions and goes into devastating action, hanging two of the school's members from a lamp post as

The Big Boss (1971): Bruce Lee.

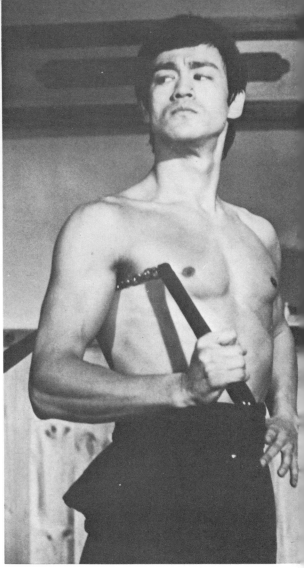

Fist of Fury (1972): Bruce Lee.

Fist of Fury: Bruce Lee is fifth from left, Robert Baker second from left, and Lo Wei sixth from left.

Fist of Fury.

a graphic warning, before going on to stage the first of his virtual on-screen tournaments with one of his ex-martial arts pupils in real life, Robert Baker, thinly disgusied as a Russian fight artist. Not every tournament is quite that authentic though – the film incorporates the usual Japanese sword-artist, and it is doubtful if Lee's 'singing rod of death' would be quite as effective in reality as it is in the film. What raises the film out of the ordinary, however, is precisely Lee's manic performance, plus those characteristic touches like the 'disguise' he uses to pose as a telephone engineer, or the flying kick with which he demolishes the sign that reads 'No Dogs or Chinese Allowed' – an image that floats out of the film becoming in a sense an emblem of the films themselves.

Lee wrote and directed as well as produced *Way of the Dragon* (1972) himself. Originally called *Enter the Dragon*, until Warners took the title for their film, he described it accurately enough in an interview: 'It is really a simple plot about a country boy going to a place where he cannot speak the language, but somehow he comes out on top by beating the hell out of anyone who comes in his way.' The film was to have been the first in a series in which Lee was to continue the character of Tang Lung. The tone is light: Lee plays a strong-arm hired by the owner of a Chinese restaurant in Rome to sort out his problems with the local syndicate. He arrives in the archetypal garb of the country Chinese clutching a bundle, and overtly mystified by the curious customs he finds in action around him. He makes great play with his role of man-without-technology, confronting the denizens of the technologically powerful West and winning hands down. He is greeted with intense scepticism wherever he goes – a scepticism banished by one flash of those superbly attuned muscles. The conflicts modulate from preliminary tussles in the restaurant itself to serious confrontations in the service area outside, and a lethal escapade involving a rooftop sniper which Tang Lung (Lee) counters by skilful use of carved wood darts. The darkest fight of all is shot partly in the Colosseum and partly in a studio mock up – a virtual contest between Chuck Norris and himself (Norris is seven times U.S. and World Karate Champion). Earlier Lee had 'demolished' Robert Wall and Wang Ing Sik – both also professional fighters. The fight with Norris, as one of the gang's heavies, ends in death following a gruesome dislocation and a blow from Lee that breaks his neck. *Way of the Dragon* is a film that shows all the roughness you would expect from a first directorial effort. It is impossible to predict from it what filmic directions Lee would have taken – except for that possibly unexpected leaning towards comedy.

Enter the Dragon (1973), which Concord (Lee's company) co-produced with Warner Brothers, incorporated a virtual army of tournament champions. Among them were its stars, John Saxon (Master of Tai Chi Chuan), Jim Kelly (Karate Champion), Robert Wall (1970 U.S. Karate Champion), Peter Archer, Yang Sze Stotoka and Angela Mao, as well as a grand total of 200 lesser lights from the fight world, all performing in the service of a fantasy along James Bond lines that in reality was nothing more than a dark throw-back to the American oriental-paranoia of twenty or even fifty years earlier. Shih Kien plays the surrogate Dr No and Lee a fight expert (called Lee) from a Shaolin temple, sent as a government agent to crack the vice and drugs ring that centres on his island fortress.

Despite the supposed Hollywood professionalism behind it all, the film remained a decidedly rough effort in

which it was left to the scenes of combat – which Lee directed himself – to save the day. One, in which Lee confronts his iron-handed villain with supreme narcissism in a mirrored maze, was certainly memorable.

Way of the Dragon (1972).

Way of the Dragon: Bruce Lee and Chuck Norris.

Way of the Dragon: Bruce Lee.

Enter the Dragon: Bruce Lee.

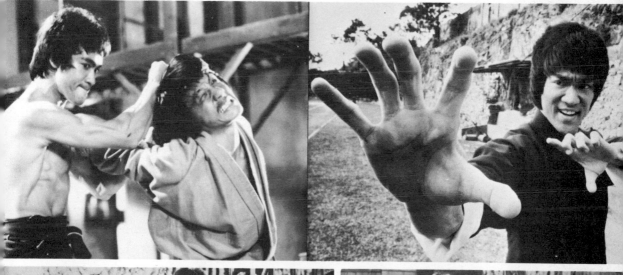

Game of Death (1973): Bruce Lee.

Lee's death left several of his projects incomplete. *Game of Death* (1973) seems to have continued the humorous if obsessive vein of *Way of the Dragon* – in it Lee, a lithe five-foot-four, confronts a seven-foot-plus Harlem Globetrotter and Karate Champion on one occasion and what looks like the Incredible Hulk on another. At the same time Lee was working on several ideas for costume films – there are stills taken of him dressed as various Chinese folk heroes, and one of him rolling his eyes unconvincingly as the Blind Swordsman Zatoichi. He was also interested in opening up the market for Cantonese films – something that both major companies seem about to put into action. In addition he took time from his own commitments to direct fight scenes for various independently made films, such as *Fist of the Unicorn*.

Lee, in common with a large number of other performers in the Hong Kong film industry, came to films through a background in Chinese opera (his father was the Cantonese actor and opera star Lee Hoi-chuen) and involvement in the then thriving Cantonese film industry. He was born in San Francisco when his parents were on tour in America. Returning to Hong Kong, Lee began to appear as a child actor in Cantonese films, in which he made a name for himself in Mickey Rooney-type roles. His first film was *Birth of a Man*. By the time he was thirteen he was already studying martial arts seriously (the Wing Chun school) although his father had earlier passed on the rudiments of *Tai Chi* to him. Lee also seems to have punctuated his film appearances, and education at St. Francis Xavier's College in Kowloon, with a fair sprinkling of back-alley tournaments of his own. For a while he commuted between the States and Hong Kong before settling down at Washington University, Seattle, where he studied philosophy and wrote a thesis on the new pared-down martial art style he originated, called *jeet kune do*. At the age of twenty-three, he married and the couple moved to Oakland, which is where, in 1964, he appeared in a karate tournament, giving a display that impressed the producer of Batman sufficiently for him to sign Lee for the series. The part of Kato in *The Green Hornet* followed (this was the part that was successfully to reintroduce him to Chinese audiences); and another in *Longstreet* in an episode called 'The Way of the Fist', in which Lee coaches the blind detective, played by James Franciscus, in the not so gentle art of *jeet kune do*. The episode received exceptionally good reviews. Then in 1968 he was given a small part in *Marlowe*, a not too imaginative version of one of Chandler's Philip Marlowe stories in which James Garner had the lead. Lee was given the opportunity of smashing up Marlowe's office, but not Marlowe himself. By this time, Lee had opened three martial arts schools and was able to command some $1,500 for a ten-hour session. Pupils included James Garner, Lee Marvin, Steve McQueen. He was friendly with Roman Polanski. There was talk of Lee perhaps being cast as Kwai Chang Caine in the original version of the television series *Kung Fu*, then known as *The Warrior*, but that came to nothing. 'I guess', Lee is quoted as remarking philosophically, 'they weren't ready for a Hopalong Wong'. Lee, in fact, was facing the kind of problem that beset black actors before the black film market was opened up.

Sometime in 1969 Hong Kong television was given a glimpse of the physique-straining, eye-testing action that within a year was to ricochet its exponent to stardom. Lee was back in Hong Kong doing an exceptionally well-publicised promotional programme for the launching of *The Green*

The Green Hornet.

Marlowe (1968): Bruce Lee and James Garner.

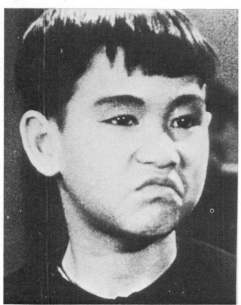

My Son A Chang (1948): Bruce Lee.

Bruce Lee, the Man and the Legend (1973).

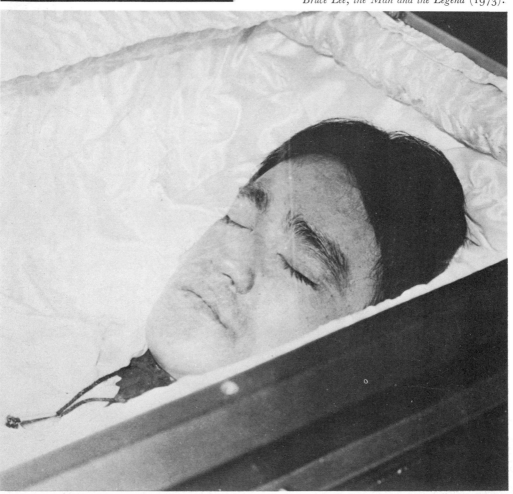

Hornet on Chinese television. The high point of the display came when he demolished three inch-thick boards suspended in the air with a single side kick. It was exactly the point at which sword-play films were resorting to ever larger doses of hand-to-hand fighting, and Raymond Chow, who had just set up Golden Harvest, was impressed enough to put Lee on contract in a film that always looked like a no-risk project. It was only after the success of *The Big Boss* that offers of multi-million dollar contracts began to stream back from the States.

My Son A-Chang is a small black and white social comedy which the – in this case – inappropriately named Elephantine Company made in the late 'forties. Set in the back-streets of Hong Kong, it has a young Bruce Lee playing the wayward nephew of a jobless teacher. The plot incorporates a series of contretemps with a high powered local businessman who puts Lee, as A-Chang, to work in his sweat-shop clothing factory where he is to live, which effectively means working day and night. He is seven years old and the astonishing thing about his performance is just how familiar it is. There are the same ploys for winning over the audience, the same set-piece fight – only this time with a broom handle – the same championing of the poor – A-Chang picks up with a gang of small-time crooks headed by one Dagger Li and makes occasional Robin Hood-like largess-donating forays back to his old slum home.

Twenty-five years later, Concord put together a hastily patched documentary which seems to have remained on the shelf. It is called *Bruce Lee the Man and the Legend* (1973) and it conspicuously fails to illuminate either. It is an attempt to present a compendium of myth-making cliches: opening on a silhouette of Linda Lee's face against a sunset over which a voice intones, 'The king of kung fu is dead', the film then proceeds to lose itself in wodges of untranslated material – like the Lee script conference which we hear on tape in Cantonese – and filler material like the footage of students from Lee's old martial arts school going through Lee's favourite postures. Through the welter of nonsequiteurs we catch an attempt to describe Lee as not only, predictably enough, a good family man (he had two children) but also, more interestingly, a defender of China and Chinese culture in the face of Western prejudice and indifference, and of course, a phenomenal martial artist. There are tales of how he mastered thirty moves in a day – something that would take an ordinary man a month. (If it is true, that alone might explain his death.) There are shots of the funeral, his children, and Linda Lee's wreath inscribed 'Until our next incarnation'. Shots of Lee as a child-actor include a curiously Keatonesque one in which he wears an enormous painted moustache. Some pseudo-reverential pans around his house give us a chance to catch – amid close-ups of 'his shoes, his belt, his dog' – the gleaming chrome temple to the great god muscle which it took, we are told, eight weeks to build. A curious picture emerges dotted with dissonant elements: the cartoon of father and son on a wall – both grotesquely be-muscled, the semi-psychedelic paintings, and although the camera moves fast, it doesn't move fast enough to prevent us reading the proclamation on a poster beneath a giant blow-up of a tiger's head: 'Patience my ass, I'm gonna kill something'.

Some of the actors who worked with him before his death describe him as a violent man, always ready to prove himself, but 'he also saw himself as the oppressed man's hero; he felt he was making it for them. But he thought people were plain stupid to let themselves be oppressed.' Apparently he felt

Fist of Fury.

Fist of Fury.

Enter the Dragon: Bruce Lee.

Enter the Dragon: Bruce Lee.

Marlowe: Bruce Lee and James Garner.

that *Enter the Dragon* had been a mistake: 'He knew his impact always lay in the fact that he was on the side of the little man, in that film he was simply an authority figure.'

Lee is outrageous. He is often very funny and more than a bit of a ham. In his films he is a superlative fighter, a balletic exponent of a deadly art, in which it is impossible to separate the deadliness from the art. He didn't have to know how to act, he had something else that for many people transformed ordinary material into the charismatic – a sense of precarious passivity in which the passivity is nothing more than a thin veneer over the dangerous. He wears his cosmetic battle scars with a physical pride that transforms mundane scenes. In *Marlowe* he was sent up, along with his fight style, and 'coped with' by James Garner as Marlowe, who non-chalantly remarks 'You're light on your feet – maybe just a little bit gay?' Thereby provoking Lee into the leap that ends in his death. Perhaps Lee had the last laugh after all, for nothing is more noticeable than his ability to make anyone else on the screen, particularly those western martial artists he delighted in trouncing, look like so much dead meat.

It is easy to see how Lee won audiences over, less easy to assess what permanent contribution he made to Chinese film beyond spawning a continuing series of look-alikes and at least one film which promises to tell it like it was about the ins and outs of his personal life. His image swings constantly between that of the little boy who upset the apple cart and the bone-hard body fanatic. Probably the truth lay somewhere between the two.

10. One-Armed Invincibility: Wang Yu

'I must avenge teacher's death. I'm responsible and I'm helpless and a cripple.'
One-armed Boxer

If Bruce Lee added grace and balletic sensuality to his depiction of violent conflict on the screen without lessening the effect of that violence, and added a cult hero to its iconography, Wang Yu framed fights that are simply the longest filmed – the climatic one in *Beach of the War Gods* (1970–3) running well over twenty minutes – and that contain a greater degree of violence against both the hero himself and the antagonists he confronts. In one film he is virtually split open but wraps his escaping entrails around him and continues

Zatoichi and the One-armed Swordsman (1970): Wang Yu.

A Man Called Tiger (1972).

fighting. In the 'One-Armed' series he not only undergoes the pain involved in loss of the limb, but also that torture attendant on building his remaining limb into a doubly strong instrument of revenge. In *The Tattooed Dragon* (1973) he undergoes a severe attack by a gang, on attempting to reclaim stolen temple funds, and spends the rest of the film first in bed and then hobbling around painfully, only throwing away his stick for the final fray. In *Ten Fingers of Steel* (1973) he is pinned under a massive boulder. In *A Man Called Tiger* (1972) he is confronted by a half-dozen strong gang, armed to a man with axes. Those who cross his path fare little better, with eye-gouging becoming almost routine in *The Chinese Boxer* (1969), along with beheadings and those knife-blade blows to the chest. There is also the personal scorched earth policy he pursues in *Golden Swallow* (*Girl with the Thunderbolt Kick*, 1969), quite apart from the normal repertory of more or less lethal kicks, chops, bone-crushing grips and groin-smashing stabs. It is this no-holds-barred attitude to fight sequences, linked to the creation of a deliberately diffident and non-heroic character, that gives his films their highly individualistic slant. In *Seaman Number Seven*, for instance, his sole motivation seems to be the persistent hope that maybe a fight – in which he will find the world working once more on his own terms – will eventuate.

Wang Yu joined Shaws in 1963 but at that time musicals overshadowed action films in popularity and it was not until 1966 that he made much impact in a small part in which he drew notice for his obvious athletic ability: he could do his own stunts and knew Chinese martial arts. He was cast by Shaws in *The One-armed Swordsman* (1968, directed by Chang Cheh) and in its sequel *The Return of the One-armed Swordsman*. This developed the classic situation in which the swordsman is discovered living peacefully in the country until an invitation to a duelling contest arrives. A local gang, here the notorious Eight Demon Swordsmen, capture all the swordsmen of the village and demand an arm from each of them as ransom, before going on to kidnap Fang's (Wang Yu) wife – at which point he duly dusts off his sword and enters the fray.

Before he left Shaws to go independent, Wang Yu was involved in several rather run-of-the-mill essays into costume heroics. One was the ill-fated *The Invincible*, but others, more interesting, were the remarkable *Golden Swallow* and the gory fight epic, *The Chinese Boxer*.

Golden Swallow is a romantic sword-fight epic, one of a string that was built around the central character of Cheng Pei Pei as the swordswoman Golden Swallow. Chang Cheh, the director, manages to weave together scenes of general explication (she and the swordsman, played by Lo Lieh, beside a waterfall, filling us in on background details) with a series of astonishing scenes in which Wang Yu, as Silver Roc, fells four men at a blow, or cuts them down in their path with China's answer to the bullet – the dart. Wang Yu traverses the film like an emblem of death – white being symbolic of death in the Chinese iconography – or, as the dialogue has it, 'He swoops down on his enemies like a silver white roc . . . no one has survived a duel with him.' If the slaughter itself is strange, the fact that he leaves behind at each scene of devastation a talisman with Golden Swallow's emblem on it is even more so. Silver Roc's multiple killings have all the desperate and stately abandon of the wayward Brando-esque or James Dean-like hero who kills as a plea for understanding. Unusually, the film takes great care to establish the characters' capability for tenderness: the scene in which Silver Roc visits the brothel and through the open window

The Chinese Boxer (1970): Wang Yu.

Golden Swallow (1969): Wang Yu.

there drifts the sound of a distraught mother mourning the death of her child, or the extraordinary sequence in which Golden Swallow visits Silver Roc at the same brothel dressed as a man. The action scenes are equally evocative: the invasion of the innermost sanctum of the Dragon Gang described quite simply in the script as 'the root of all evil', in which a solid wall of soldiers suddenly cut Silver Roc off from his friends; the battle on ground that suddenly gives way to an array of sharpened stakes; the scene of combat in which each slash of Silver Roc's sword brings down a wall of corpses; and finally the fraught duel in which Silver Roc is killed through a tragic mistake and dies insisting to the end, in common with those death figures of the American gangster movies, that he is still 'the supreme swordsman' and 'invincible'. Wang Yu performs with a great sense of fatality, great charisma and just the degree of masochism the character requires.

Zatoichi and the One-armed Swordsman

Golden Swallow: Wang Yu.

Zatoichi and the One-armed Swordsman: Wang Yu.

(1970), although not the last of the series (David Chiang was to re-create the part for Shaws a few years later), was the last in which Wang Yu was involved, and it is also by far the best. In it Wang Yu is teamed with Shintaro Katsu, playing once more the great blind folk hero samurai of Japanese cinema, Zatoichi. If the film is notably less tough-minded than the Japanese original, it is still one of the all-time masterpieces of Chinese, or Sino-Japanese, cinema. In this essay on the

implications of blindnesses of various kinds, Wang Yu plays a Chinese wandering through Japan who finds his path crosses that of a Chinese touring circus. He follows them on the road, only to find himself witness to the sudden mindless slaughter of the whole family in the midst of a stately funeral procession gone mad. Fleeing with the sole survivor, a young child, he finds himself accused of the killings and becomes a hunted man; but he also finds his path dogged by the rough samurai Li who maintains a pose as a

Zatoichi and the One-armed Swordsman.

Zatoichi and the One-armed Swordsman.

The Chinese Boxer: Wang Ping and Wang Yu.

masseur. Enmity grows to friendship, as Blind Li, through a system of careful strategies, discovers the identity of the true villains and kills them. Throughout, deliberately terse dialogue is played off against visuals that explore the devious motivations behind the characters' action with great suggestiveness. Blind Li, the by-the-end-of-the-film emotionally blind Fang (Wang Yu), and the extraordinary geisha who watches from the sidelines, are observed with totally unsentimental warmth. Blind Li and Fang are a strange supernatural pair and Wang Yu establishes for himself a character who is almost as great a mystery as the blind man who 'sees'. *Zatoichi and the One-armed Swordsman* is realized with rare boldness of vision – whether it is Wang Yu's miraculous tree-top flight, child in arms, the deeper insight suggested by the blind man's curious gestures and movements (always pictured as they were in the original in intense close-up), or the deeper wisdom hinted at in the sequence of two blind men playing dice together.

In these films can be found all the gestures that were to become stunted and graceless in the more blatant scissors-and-paste jobs Wang Yu subsequently found himself involved with.

Before he severed his connections with Shaws, Wang Yu was to try his hand at directing and writing. The film, *The Chinese Boxer*, is a revenge tale writ characteristically large – the acts of aggression against Lei's (Wang Yu) martial arts school involves not just one or two deaths, but the extermination of the whole school. Lei is only spared because he is knocked out early on and left for dead amid the carnage. The film uses all the basic motifs of the Chinese action film: the threatened martial arts school, wise words from the teacher, impatience and rebelliousness from Lei, the gone-bad martial artist who returns to town with his Japanese

The Beach of the War Gods (1970/73).

karate killers (one played by Lo Lieh), the 'special technique' (here it is the iron palm), and those scenes of desperate practice for revenge. In concentrating all these elements into one film, Wang Yu achieves a perfect cross between the one-armed series and the typical 'rival schools' film. For, as in the earlier series, Lei passes from being the school's top fighter to complete impotence, out of which he is only gradually, and with much physical hardship, nursed.

Apart from the curious notion of having Wang Yu as Lei spend a good part of the film with what looks like a doctor's mask over his face as, presumably, an extemporised disguise, from a visual point of view the film is decidedly bracing. It is not so much the way in which particular shots are set up, as in the bold movement from shot to shot. For instance, a group of karate experts descend on an inn and in quick succession one crushes a glass between his fingers to demand service, threatens to tear the place apart, delivers a

karate chop to the table to prove his point, splitting it in half as he does so, escalates upwards in a massive leap that lifts the tiles, descends on the other side of the room before a hapless Chinese, gouges out his eyes and leaves him dead on the floor.

Similarly, instead of playing the 'iron fist' section straight, Wang Yu places the cauldron of iron filings in a cave, where he is surrounded by gruesome masks over which the firelight plays suggestively, where the air rings with distorted laughter; nothing if not a glutton for physical punishment, he closes his body-building sequence with a few shots of himself jumping up and down with rocks tied to his feet. Characteristically, too, it is the gang's gall in having a friend of his put in prison for allegedly using a weighted dice, and the leader taking the opportunity to rape (on screen) his wife, that proves the final straw which precipitates us into the real fighting. In it, Wang Yu makes sure he is confronted

The Beach of the War Gods.

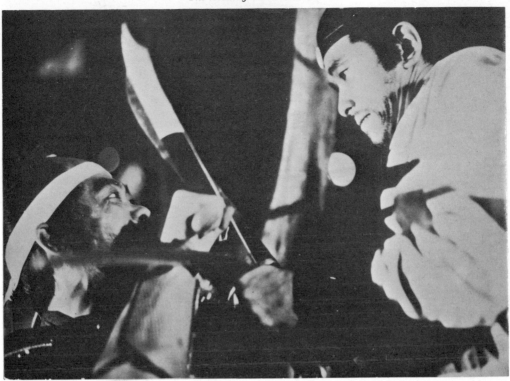

by every conceivable weapon, and uses every conceivable martial arts technique in retaliation, turning each assailant's weapon against himself in an outright fight-feast. In the final conflict he is tricked, but even this cannot prevent him turning a couple of disorientating somersaults before laying the Japanese karate expert to rest and dying himself.

The second major film he was to direct himself, *Beach of the War Gods*, was an epic replay of *The Magnificent Seven* against a background of Japanese incursions into Chinese territory during the Ming dynasty. Wang Yu plays the famous Chinese fighter and patriot called Hsiao Feng as a cross between a Toshiro Mifune-type samurai and a lone Western hero in the Eastwood mould. Again he shows a lot of skill in keeping the vast project – it is of epic dimensions – afloat and in filling the screen with images of great boldness. There is another sequence involving

masks and dancing firelight: this time the Japanese army's booby-trapped progress up the beach that gives the film its title. The film ends with the famous twenty-minute climactic battle scene, at the end of which the Chinese army moves on, leaving a solitary figure still standing; they advance and pass him by, moving to one side of the screen, while he slowly falls dead to the other. It is ridiculous, and extreme and effective. There are, too, some fine incidental characters, such as the waxy-faced mercenary whose chest is criss-crossed with loaded knife belts. But then again, you come down to a script written by Wang Yu himself that is so extraordinarily anti-Japanese that it seems at odds with a film that never stoops to the grotesque caricature the dialogue suggests. If the visuals are frequently comic-strip in the sense that they are clear and uncompromisingly dynamic, the script is comic-strip in the sense that it remains an extended war-cry.

The One-armed Boxer (1970/71).

The One-armed Boxer: Wang Yu.

At the end of 1970, Wang Yu directed *The One-armed Boxer*, the tournament film mentioned earlier, that is probably the most audacious of the lot. Again he wrote the script and took the part of the invincible one-armed boxer, the martial arts school's most impatient pupil, who projects it into a state of war by his extra-curricular fighting. The villain of the piece, Shao, recruits a whole retinue of exotic fighters. In the ensuing fight Yu (Wang Yu) loses an arm, but with the help of a herbalist learns the iron fist technique. 'We will have to kill all the nerves in the arm', the old man explains, opening a large and ancient jar, 'if even one remains, it won't work'. The old man also tells him about the 600 pressure points. The almost constant round of fights is played off with a vigorous sense of inventiveness. He twice confronts his exotic array of fight experts including the inflatable lamas, the rough *taekwondo* fighter, the twin Thai boxers, the fanged Japanese karate master and the Indian yogi, whose speciality is circling his opponent, walking on his hands at an ever-increasing rate. The imperturbable Wang Yu, of course, goes one better, when unforgettably he does the same on one finger. With this film, blow by blow enaction of tournament-style fights is mingled with a feeling for the rare and strange in a way that benefits both elements as well as the basic revenge story at its core. *The One-armed Boxer* is one of the best and most action-packed films to have come out of the Hong Kong film industry.

In *The Big Boss*, Bruce Lee as the young factory worker Cheng confronted the head of the dope ring and defeated him single-handed. In *Seaman Number Seven* (*Wang Yu's Seven Magnificent Fights*), Wang Yu plays a deliberately laconic sailor with a penchant for whistling the 'Bridge on the River Kwai March', and a distinctly throwaway manner, who finds himself stowing

The One-armed Boxer.

away on a ship bound for Japan and some big-time illegal drug deals. This serves as the basic situation to bring Wang (the character's name) into confrontation with, first the humbler members of the gang, and then the top men who don't draw the line at murdering Wang's uncle and friends. Everything else in the film disappears beneath a series of fights that are again not only expert but viscerally involving, as they shift absurdly from land to water and back. The underwater sequence is, in fact, hauntingly claustrophobic and the final fight-out with the bleached blond 'Big Boss' and his

sumo wrestlers concludes this outrageous and generally good-humoured film with the kind of dynamism you would expect. Lo Wei directed it and stitches himself into a small part as a waiter.

Wang Yu's latest film, again made for an independent company, First Scope, units four Chinese heavies in an action drama called *Four Real Friends* (1974). One of the friends is the ubiquitous Chen Hsing (an ex-Shaw actor) who also turns up in *Kung Fu the Headcrusher* as the invincible investigator.

The One-armed Boxer.

11. Swords of Death: David Chiang & Ti Lung

'He's killed the Killer!'
Duel of Fists/The Chinese Connection

The bulk of action films produced by Shaws since 1968 have been traditional sword-wielding costume dramas. The most reliable money-spinners among them have been produced by a single unit working virtually as a repertory company within the studio, a nucleus of actors and technicians that collected around director Chang Cheh. One of Chang Cheh's early action films was the original *One-armed Swordsman*. He directed the sequel as well as *Golden Swallow (Girl with the Thunderbolt Kick)*. After Wang Yu left Shaws, Chang Cheh brought into the studio on contract two eighteen-year-old stuntmen he had been working with for several years and to whom he had already given small parts in his films. They were David Chiang and Ti Lung and they provided the acting nucleus of a unit that, with script writer I Kuang and cameraman Kung Mu-to, fed the action-hungry market for six years. The films virtually annexed the world of dynastic strife and knightly heroism in Shaw Brothers' rather pessimistic mode, turning aside from time to time to dispense fist-to-fist style action in the more contemporary world of singer-killers and gang warfare.

Stylistically the films are often uneven: moments of ornate pomp alternate with inexplicable jumps in the storyline, or, the last resort, the narra-voice-over is used to patch together unrelated incidents which may or may not be exciting in themselves. None of

Chang Cheh.

The Pirate (1972): Ti Lung (left) and David Chiang.

The Deadly Duo (1971): Ti Lung (left) and David Chiang.

that matters too much alongside the ingenuousness with which David Chiang and Ti Lung walk through their respective parts as betrayed and betrayer, friend and foe, ally, henchman, hanger-on or brothers-in-arms.

Bruce Lee criticised Chinese films for their 'unreality' and the climactic fight scenes in the Shaw action movies rely not only on their leading actors' skill in martial arts but also on trick photography, hoists and pulleys, and the ever-present trampoline for those impossible leaps . . . in fact every aid to super explicitness and artificiality is deliberately embraced.

If the films are reminiscent of anything in Western film-making, it is probably either those Italian costume dramas in which Hercules confronted various exotic evil-doers, or the vein of Hollywood swashbucklers that enjoyed vast popularity during the 'forties and 'fifties. Shaws epics, in fact, are individual films only nominally: they function like serials – the names may change but the characters are recognizable from film to film (as are the costumes and sets). Our heroes (or, more rarely, heroines) set out in reel 1 to confront yet another conundrum in one or other distant dynasty, pursue their goal through an environment fraught with various hazards only to leave their heroic mark on events at the penultimate moment. The extraordinary thing to those brought up on the adventures of invincible comic book heroes is that, as often as not, they die plunging off on suicide missions, giving the films a curiously pessimistic undertone.

The first film the duo found themselves involved in was a contemporary social drama called *Dead End* (1968). Ti Lung plays an office worker who is fired for bringing a girl back to the office at night; David Chiang plays his friend. They find themselves in conflict with the girl's minor gangster brother, a situation that escalates to murder and death at the hands of the police.

In *Have Sword Will Travel* (1969), Ti Lung plays a swordsman hired to escort a load of treasure to a neighbouring town and David Chiang, the mystery knight they take for a spy, but who in fact dies trying to save them. In *The Heroic Ones* (1970), David Chiang's paranoid intensity was played off against the rest in a tale of double-cross between brothers (Ti Lung is one) manipulated by rival warlords. By the time of *White Water Strand*, one of a trilogy of tales in a film called *Trilogy of Swordsmanship* (1971), each was given the opportunity to rescue the other in an environment of ambush, mistaken motives and knightly nobility.

Have Sword Will Travel (1969): David Chiang.

A burst of popularity for the 'twenties gangster movie resulted in *The Duel* (1969), in which David Chiang again plays the part of a man mistaken for a killer, only to prove his loyalties in the nick of time, and, more interestingly, *Vengeance* (1970). Set in the period when China was painfully and disastrously torn apart by warring rival warlords, the film contained, within its highly fraught plot and stifling sets, in which the effect of the action was anything but cathartic, a series of graphic maimings and slayings. It opens in a theatre. Ti Lung as the actor Yu-lan is caught in the middle of performing a ritualistic stage killing. He is pre-

cipitated into a real life situation in which he seeks to avenge himself on the leader of a faction that has its base in a martial arts school. He is killed. Cue for entrance of the avenging brother – and David Chiang gives the part of the self-righteous avenger a rare pathological obsessiveness – whether summarily executing both his brother's wife and the man he discovers in her bed, or turning the supposed site of his own death into a scene of unrelieved carnage. Finally, the avenger himself is mortally wounded in a shot which Chang Cheh turns into a whole choreography of death as he leaps down the staircase, blood cascading from a wound, to fight on,

The Duel (1969): David Chiang.

Vengeance (1970): Ti Lung.

before himself dying, while we cut to a bland shot of a woman waiting at the cross-roads under the apple blossom. The sheer accumulation of graphically portrayed death and disaster and its meticulous charting of a world of corruption take the film to the level of Jacobean tragedy . . . closing clichés and all. *Vengeance* won David Chiang the Best Actor award at the Asian Film Festival but, unfortunately, has had no exposure abroad. The highly effective motif of violence as an explosion of frustration in deliberately and claustophobically rectilinear confines returns again later in *The Boxer From Shantung* (1971), in which the would-be champion's dreams of a quick fortune to be

made at Shantung collapse.

By 1970, with Wang Yu hard at work at Golden Harvest on his various one-armed sequels, it was obviously time for Shaws to see what they could make of the handicapped hero. Chang Cheh cast David Chiang as the once over bold swordsman Lei Li, who cuts off his own arm after suffering defeat at the hands of a false martial arts master. Ti Lung plays the flawless swordsman who discovers him in self-imposed banishment working as a waiter in a run-down country inn and lures him back into the world again. 'Ordinary people are happier than swordsmen', he asserts at one point, but no one believes it for a moment.

The Boxer from Shantung (1971): Chen Kuan-tai.

The New One-armed Swordsman (1970): Ti Lung.

The New One-armed Swordsman: David Chiang.

The film hinges on two enormous one-against-the-multitude set-pieces. The first occurs when Ti Lung as Feng invades Tiger Fort, penetrating its innermost fastnesses only to find himself the object of an elaborate hoax from which there is only one way out – a fight to the death in a hall full of armed guards, that only ends when his body is strung up from the roof and hacked in two. The second occurs when Lei Li invades the same fort and turns himself into a cross between a sleight-of-hand artist and death machine, finally breaking through the martial artist's iron solid defence. The film repeats the earlier version's preoccupation with Lei Li's juggling stunts at the inn, and Chang Cheh animates the fights with a vigorous use of zoom shots. There are some excellent transitions – the shot of the severed arm pinned to a tree which is followed by a slow pan to take in changing seasons, before the camera moves back to reveal that now only whitened bones hang from the trunk. Chang Cheh, too, is obviously fascinated with the central relationship between the two swordsmen, the sleek and smiling Feng on one hand, the tense withdrawn Lei Li on the other, and he gives it unexpectedly subtle overtones. Where Wang Yu's one-armed fighter resolves his position of being at a touchingly noticeable disadvantage in a contentious world through hard training, an acceptance of a fair degree of masochism, and down-to-earth bloody-mindedness, David Chiang's one-armed swordsman finds himself faced with a puzzle of almost mythic dimensions – how to defeat a man whose supremely skilful use of a certain weapon makes him all-but invincible in man-to-man combat, even when the man he fights isn't crippled.

Sometimes the *raison d'être* of *Deadly Duo* (1971) seems to be the opportunity it gives Ti Lung to strip to the waist and athletically wield a double-headed axe

The Deadly Duo: Ti Lung and Ku Feng.

against all-comers, but it also repeats the situation in which David Chiang plays the fraught *alter ego* to Ti Lung's straightman. Primitive heroism has a field day, lacing the film with such supernatural elements as characters labelled Fire, Earth and Tree men, and feats of derring-do, in which characters pluck handfuls of arrows from the air before they reach their target. The changes are wrought on the scenes of swordplay and hatchet work, too, by equipping David Chiang with a sophisticated harpoon-like weapon of deadly propensities. It all ends with Chiang, already smitten with a fatal wound, holding the bridge against all comers, while Ti Lung helps his rescued Prince to safety. More of the same turned up in *The Pirate* (1972), in which good use was made of Shaws' studio beach. In it, Ti Lung has an opportunity to be misunderstood as the Robin Hood-like pirate who attempts to free local villagers from the oppressive rule of a tyrant. (David Chiang plays the distrustful minor official who is only gradually won round.)

Blood Brothers (*Chinese Vengeance*, 1972) is more ambitious in its deliberate playing off of the characters of three very different men – introducing Chen Kuan Tai as a kind of dissolute young innocent into the double act. Briefly, a drop-out from the imperial promotional system is held up by two highwaymen and ends by joining them, but not before he has converted them to his idealistic credo of positive action. They band together and build themselves a

The Deadly Duo: Ti Lung.

The Deadly Duo: Ti Lung.

The Pirate: Ti Lung.

Blood Brothers (1972).

private army, but the tensions between the men begin to show, exacerbated by the presence of Huang's (Chen Kuan Tai) wife. Years later Ma (Ti Lung), now a famous general in a precariously lofty position, invites his blood brothers to join him. They do, with their private army, and a collage of battle scenes follows. However, love once more intervenes and Ma is tempted to use his power to eliminate the weakest and most innocent of the band – which he does. Chang (David Chiang) discovers what has happened and puts into action a bold assassination plan which involves precipitating himself into the midst of the General's court and duelling to the death. The film comes unstuck, predictably, in its coy handling of the romance.

By 1973 it takes less than a sixth sense to divine a creeping impatience with the sheer weight of Shaws' studio sets and lavish period costumes. In *All Men Are Brothers* (1973), any attempt to make a coherent narrative out of the handful of essentially separate heroic confrontations is jettisoned, leaving Chang Cheh attempting to lift the seemingly unshiftable weight through vigorous use of zoom shots, rapid cuts and lightning pans. What remains is a series of fantastic and heroically primitive battle scenes that inevitably culminate in sharp and visually effective images of death and defeat, regardless of the wrap-up script. One hero, for instance, anchored half in and half out of the water by the grid of a castle gate that descends and pins him there, is pincushioned with arrows. Chang Cheh films it directly from above in a persuasive image of futility. Or there is Chen Kuan-tai at the end of an extended battle on a hill in which he is seriously outnumbered, pausing to wipe the patently imitation 'house' blood from his tattooed torso with the words, 'Take a good look at who you have

Blood Brothers: David Chiang.

killed . . . I am the Tattooed Dragon!' before falling down dead. Again, to take a different aspect of the film, the superb opening sequence in which the Emperor's courtesan offers him a gift: a musician playing, head-bowed, behind a carefully draped curtain, a musician who is a renegade, and also, as we have gathered from the first scene, the courtesan's lover. Very ambiguous, very subtle.

The motif of small-time gangland struggles that characterized David Chiang's and Ti Lung's first film with Shaws was carried over into *The Singing Killers* (1970), in which David Chiang played a nightclub singer forced back into his former life of crime. The all-pervasive world of organized crime appeared too in an invigorating diversion called *Duel of Fists* (*Chinese Connection*, 1971). A camp effort, it involves

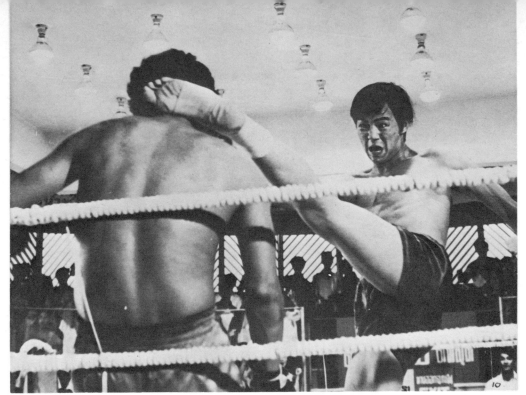

Duel of Fists (1971).

The Angry Guest (1971):
David Chiang.

The Generation Gap (1972).

a Pimpernel-type search in the gang-controlled world of Thai boxing for a long-lost brother identifiable only by a strange tattoo he has on one arm. For all its outrageously zappy clothes and riotously clichéd plotlines, the film is able to establish and hold interest through a series of neatly caught incidental details: the aide in the boxing ring with a skull and cross bones embroidered on his jacket, the ordinary warehouses that form the background to a key confrontation, complete with a truck loaded with goods going about its business unconcerned, the plump European relaxing on the balcony of a hotel during another scene, the absurd rituals of the Thai Water Festival that just happens to be in full swing during the search, and, best of all, the absolutely convincing character of the alcoholic ex-fighter who haunts the arena and delivers only slightly premature obituaries on each Thai boxer billed opposite 'The Killer'.

Duel of Fists, made the same year as Lee's *The Big Boss*, offers a series of all-out hand-to-hand fights that are choreographed with notable enthusiasm all the way from boxing ring to luxury mansion and back. The fights are lithe and powerful and shot, for once, with a keen eye for the mock heroics of the situation as well as for the latent grim realities behind it all. Ti Lung plays the fighting brother driven to go for the highest stakes by having to find sufficient money to pay for his mother's operation.

A sequel was shot in the same year. Called *The Angry Guest*, it settles the brothers from the earlier film back in Hong Kong, where one keeps an eye on the martial arts school, while the other bustles round a building site as an engineer. The film does not manage to add much to the earlier effort, apart from giving Chang Cheh the opportunity to play a crime king of Bondian proportions who demands the ultimate

price for failed missions. It does, however, finally get round to setting up that all-stops-out fight on the building site which also puts in a brief appearance in *Duel of Fists:* the workers strip off work-shirts to reveal martial arts tee-shirts underneath before moving into the attack.

The bulk of the other present-day dramas the group made at Shaws were a strange mixture of gangster films and generation-gap melodramas. There is a film actually called *The Generation Gap* (1972), in which youthful growing pains end in gangsterism and death. Another is *Friends* (1973–4), which David Chiang made as one of his last films for Shaws. He appears as an artist who rescues a friend from a gang kidnap only to earn parental disapproval. In *Young People* (1971), we are treated to kung fu in the novel context of student life with the head of the music group confronting both the basketball hero and the leader of 'The Dagger Team'.

Early in 1973 Chang Cheh, Ti Lung and David Chiang left Shaws to set up their own independent company. They immediately put into action a twelve-film production programme in which both actors would get an opportunity to script, act and direct their own films, casting actors and actresses of their choice, while Chang Cheh directed his own films and acted as producer of the others. David Chiang came back to Shaws on a one-film basis to make *The Legend of the Seven Golden Vampires* (1973–4) in which Peter Cushing's Van Helsing travels to China to trace a suspected link between Dracula and the legend of the seven golden vampires. In this he is aided by Hsi Ching (David Chiang), his sister (Shih Szu), and his six brothers – all dedicated martial artists. The film is directed by Roy Ward Baker, and is the most promising of the co-production films that have been set up to date.

Chang Cheh wrapped up his Shaw

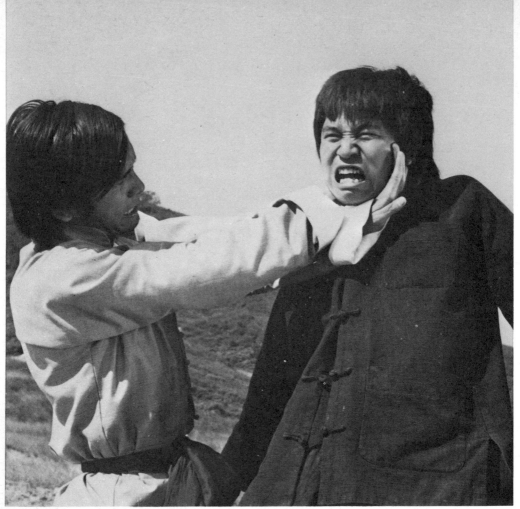

The Legend of the Seven Golden Vampires (1973/74): David Chiang.

The Legend of the Seven Golden Vampires: David Chiang.

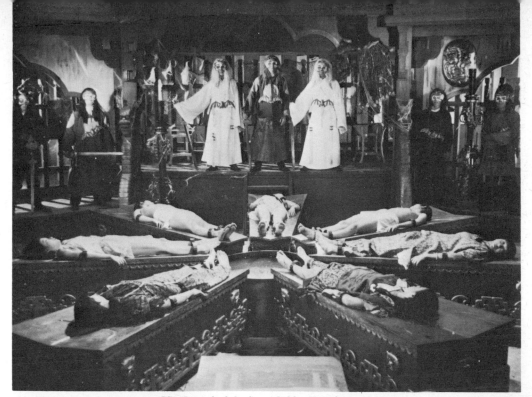

The Legend of the Seven Golden Vampires.

contract with a film that eased Chen Kuan Tai into the Ti Lung role as a bandit who changes his ways. Ti Lung was cast in the other half of the Hammer double *Shatter*, a thriller originally to be directed by Monte Hellman, but finally shot by Michael Carreras.

It is notable that once independent Chang Cheh in fact stayed with historical subjects. *Heroes Two*, made with two actors borrowed from Shaws, continued his interest in the visual romanticism of period adventures. His second, *Na Cha*, delved even further back into China's legendary past to come up with a fresh version of the often filmed adventures of the mythical hero of the title who was able to fly with the aid of fire wheels. In this episode he kills the son of a sea god who has been using his supernatural powers to inflict suffering.

David Chiang and Ti Lung, however, went into immediate reaction against their studio heroics of the last half-dozen years and set about a series of films with decidedly social leanings, although not without action. David Chiang directed Ti Lung in *The Drug Addict;* Ti Lung directed David Chiang in *The Apprentice* and himself in *Motorcycle*. By mid-1974 Chang Cheh's was one of the few financially sound independent film companies in Hong Kong; it only remained to be seen how the newly straitened circumstances would affect the films they were to make.

Shatter (1974).

12. The Final Blow

The Shadow Boxer (1973/74): Shih Szu (right) and Frankie Wei.

By the beginning of 1974 it seemed that the height of the boom had passed for the Hong Kong-based Chinese film industry. Cinemas in Hong Kong itself were feeling the pinch as a result of rising land values and were beginning to face the alternatives of closure or raising seat prices. Audience figures, though still high by world standards, were on a downswing. Television was proving a serious rival in Taiwan. Thailand had instituted a quota system for the import of foreign films. Censorship was erratic in Singapore. And the world market, so fiercely stormed in 1972 and 1973, was, only a year later, the victim of a glut that all but returned the price that the average Chinese film could command down to pre-boom level.

By March, hundreds of independent film companies had shut up shop till times should prove more auspicious. Only ten independent features were in production and only two independent companies remained both wholeheartedly involved in the action film and financially unshaken. They were the First Motion Picture Company and Chang Cheh's Film Company. Film makers found themselves without a sure-fire formula for box-office success.

Shaws set about releasing the action films they had made at the end of the

The Shadow Boxer: Shih Szu and Frankie Wei.

Supermen Against the Orient (1973): Sal Borgese, Cantafora, Shih Szu, Lo Lieh and Robert Ross.

year: *The Shadow Boxer* in which Chen Wo Fu played a road worker and kung fu expert (Chen Wo Fu, the 1971 South-east Asian Chinese Boxing Champion, died soon after the film was finished), *Iron Bodyguard*, a Chen Kuan-Tai costume adventure, and the films they had co-produced with foreign companies: *This Time I'll Make You Rich* and *Supermen Against the Orient;* they set up a number of new projects, such as *Supermen Against the Amazons* and *Virgins of the Seven Seas*. Meanwhile, they turned the direction of the bulk of their output to sex and comedy and mixtures of the two in films like *Sugar Daddies, The Killer Snakes, Kidnap, Queen Hustlers*

Supermen Against the Orient: Shih Szu.

The Killer Snakes (1973).

and *Sex Maniacs*, plus a new version of the Chinese erotic classic *Golden Lotus*. More interestingly, they began to revive the recently neglected genre of fantasy-horror with *The Ghost Lovers*, a joint Shaw-Korean venture in which the ghost of a dead woman returns to haunt her lover. At the action end of the market they produced their own version of yet another episode from the life of the Cantonese boxer Huang Fei Hung (Golden Harvest had beaten them to this particular subject though with *Skyhawk*). Shaws' internationally-cast *Bamboo House of Dolls* was awarded an unusual amount of publicity; it had Lo Lieh playing the resident good Chinese in a Japanese women's prisoner of war camp. They also had three sword films in the pipeline for international release: *Sacred Knights of Vengeance*, *Nine Blows of the Dragon* and *Shanghai Lil and the Sunlump Kid*. The main questions hanging over the company however were how long Run Run Shaw would be able to maintain control over the company, when he would cede control to one of his European-educated sons and what, if any, changes of direction that would entail. Meanwhile Shaws, not unaffected by the set-back, proceeded to cut back on two groups of employees which, practically, they found most disposable – the high-paid stars, and the technicians and studio workers.

Golden Harvest caught the end of the action market with *The Manchu Boxer* and *The Shaolin Boxer*, two home-manufactured action films, but were clearly banking on the success of Lo Wei's three projects in the States: *Back Alley Princess in Chinatown* (*The Chinese Enforcers*), a comedy continuing the adventures of the 'back-alley princess' in San Francisco; and a police thriller called *The Yellow-faced Tiger*, starring a Chinese cop played by a new actor, Wong Tao, whom they were hoping to slide into Bruce Lee's shoes.

The Bamboo House of Dolls (1973).

Yellow-faced Tiger (1973/74).

There is no doubt that Bruce Lee's death was a blow to the company, but there is the suspicion that had he lived he may well have left to seek greater freedom than Golden Harvest could offer.

Casting about for an alternative to kung fu movies, the independents, like Shaws, were turning to sex comedies or more or less worthy melodramas such as *The Wedding* or *Spring Comes Not Again* or *Father, Husband, Son*. The latter traces the life of a woman against the background of Chinese history and shows her betrayed at each point by the men in her life – her father is a rabid destructive warlord, her husband tries to sell out to the Japanese and so on. At the same time they were leaking as many of their action films out into the world market as possible. Some of them, like *Bloody Fists*, had been made a year or so earlier, and others, such as *Kung*

Fu Brothers in the Wild West, had a suitably international flavour. Also in the pipeline were several hopeful cross-genre products – kung fu plus 'sex' footage in *Adventure in Denmark* for instance, which has a young martial artist winning a prize trip to Copenhagen and being rescued from pursuing gang enmities by the inevitable Ingrid. It was directed by Ho Fan and produced by Victor Lam.

Locally, complaints were voiced about the 'arrested development' of the Chinese film. They stopped, one writer argued, at a point where 'scholars romance with fairies, cruel mothers-in-law quarrel with sweet daughters-in-law, and the rich man encounters difficulties in marrying the singer and/or the village girl'. Adaptations from modern novels were found just as bad: 'all endless suffering and death for the sake of love alternating with schoolgirl

Adventure in Denmark (1973).

fantasies of unfaithful white knights holding their fair lady in death. They have no connection with the world we live in.' This point is echoed by David Chiang: 'I want to make a film that has no violence in it, no sex, nothing. I want to tell Hong Kong people what they are, what they are doing. The audience is there, they know when a film is good, when they see something they recognise and when it is false they laugh or hiss the screen. I have lived in Hong Kong all my life and there are many things that aren't right, the gap between the rich and the poor, the corruption, the rich who steal, the businessmen who already have so many wives but have to find a different prostitute every night . . . the poor who get hooked on drugs. The swordfight film is all heroes and killing, you have to kill and you always win. Real people can't do that.'

The 'sixties in fact had, as Run Run Shaw pointed out, seen a revival of interest in the action film, an interest catered for first by obviously cribbed versions of Western films and gradually an increasing and sometimes extremely rewarding resurrections of the sword-play film. With the 'seventies, the fantastic elements of the genre were honed away by ever-increasing realistic bouts of conflict on one hand and on the other the development of an even barer almost stark forum, within which the classic Chinese codes of restraint, asceticism and patience were articulated. Probably in the end it was these films that were the 'newest', the most original; for, for all Run Run Shaw's protestation of his company's gratification of the audience's lust for 'something new', Shaws itself tended to offer little beyond variations on the tried and tested. Meanwhile working under enomous pressure, several independent companies had made films that, invariably shot either on location or in tiny ramshackle studios, achieved a blend of the *ad hoc* and the accidental that sometimes carried a freshness and a lively 'street feel' denied to those working with a more regulated framework. Of the contribution of actors turned directors – Wang Yu can be seen to have brilliantly anticipated and prepared the way for Lee's tournament dominated, comic, 'open line to the audience' style.

And the kung fu film? Even the most devoted fan recognises the terrible dubbing, the creaking conventions, the ill-matched studio shots, the random cuts made by censors at climactic points in the action, destroying at one fell swoop the whole impact of a scene . . . but the films met with vast popular support nevertheless, in the period sword films and especially in the back-alley fight or tournament films. They presented action as it had never been presented before, and they presented it in an environment that was diagrammatically clear; in them one person, without technology, without money, without power, could confront the organisation, the protection racket king, and hit back. Perhaps they were simple fantasies of power, for they showed the character who, for decades, had just been one of the crowd in Western films taking control of his or her environment in no uncertain terms and in the most direct way possible.

For the western audience, their flamboyancc broke with the arid bitterness of the American television-influence thriller and returned us to the swashbuckling fantasies of the costume film of twenty or thirty years before. They took the style of the comic-strip hero, the Crimson Avenger, or the Star Spangled Kid and returned it to us a little changed as the Little Dragon, the One-Armed Boxer, the Tattooed Dragon and the Blade that Spares None.

TITLE INDEX